Easy Sculpted Foam
for your home

Koren Russell

Published by

 **kp** **krause publications**
An F&W Publications Company

700 East State Street • Iola, WI 54990-0001
715-445-2214 • 888-457-2873
www.krause.com

To place an order or obtain a free catalog, please call 800-258-0929.

Library of Congress Catalog Number 2003110461
ISBN 0-87349-599-3

Edited by Christine Townsend
Designed by Donna Mummery
Photography by Robert Best

Dedication

To my family and friends for encouraging, sharing, tolerating, and listening.

Contents

Introduction

I had always envied clay sculptors. I was drawn to their booths at art shows, gazing in awe of what they could create. Sometimes, when my budget would allow for it, I bought clay pieces to admire at home. But it wasn't enough. I wanted to do what *they* could do.

"I *can* do this," I said to encourage myself, and I had a plan of attack: I would start by creating a round clay ball. Hours later, I still didn't have anything that resembled round. I am lopsided through and through.

Form wasn't my only difficulty. There was the problem of countless supplies, including a cost-prohibitive kiln. There are shops in the area that would have fired my pieces, but this brought out another flaw of mine: impatience.

This flaw also prohibited the long process of learning about different glazes, clays, and techniques. A technique was needed that used some of the knowledge I already had—general crafting and painting. Could these skills relate to sculpting?

One day, a challenge came my way, along with a bit of a miracle. I needed a large, chunky candleholder to show off a candle wrap in a magazine photo. Since I couldn't afford what I found, or get what I could afford quickly enough, I was forced to create something.

As miracles go, I had a package of Creative Paperclay® on hand. It was laying in a drawer waiting for a moment such as this. My kids had some foam left over from a project. (That's how I had always looked at foam—as a kid's project.) With only the supplies of a bread knife, paperclay, and stolen foam, the playing began. And the result was the discovery of a whole new world of fun and endless possibilities.

Using this Book

The first chapter explains the details needed to create the sculptures. I would suggest reading through it before starting your first creation. You will find things there that aren't detailed in the individual instructions.

Each project chapter starts with easier projects and winds up with the more difficult. The projects are rated as Easy, Medium, and Advanced. To be rated as Easy, the project needs to have simple techniques in both the shaping of the foam and covering it. With a Medium project, either the shaping or the covering will take a bit more skill. When rated as Advanced, both the shaping and covering are more skilled.

The more advanced the project, the more time it is going to take. Even the easy projects can't be considered *quick* and easy. Sculpting is a form of art; it should be a fun and enjoyable experience, not hurried along. I built in natural starting and stopping points in each project: First, the foam is shaped. If glue is needed, the creation has to be set aside for a bit. Then the form is covered. You can stop this part at any time and set it aside for later. Once it is covered, you can take another break while it dries. Any sanding is completed and, lastly, the creation is painted. It is nice to be able to create in a leisurely fashion. But if leisurely just doesn't fit your schedule, the shortest drying times are listed, as well as ways to hurry the process along.

Don't be afraid of the Advanced projects. Just work through a few of the simpler projects to get some experience. Or, if you are adventurous, dive right in. None of these creations are meant to be perfect—after all, they originated from a lopsided person! Think of imperfections as personality, signs of the hand-made touch.

Don't be afraid to do some mixing. Would you like to see the Cow Herd painted like Drake the Dinosaur? Just follow the painting instructions for Drake. How about making one of the Cow Herd as big as Colonel Sanders? Simply enlarge the patterns and start with a bigger ball.

A Gallery appears at the end of this book, where creations are pictured for inspiration. There aren't instructions for these pieces, but if you look through the book, you will find similar creations to use as a guide.

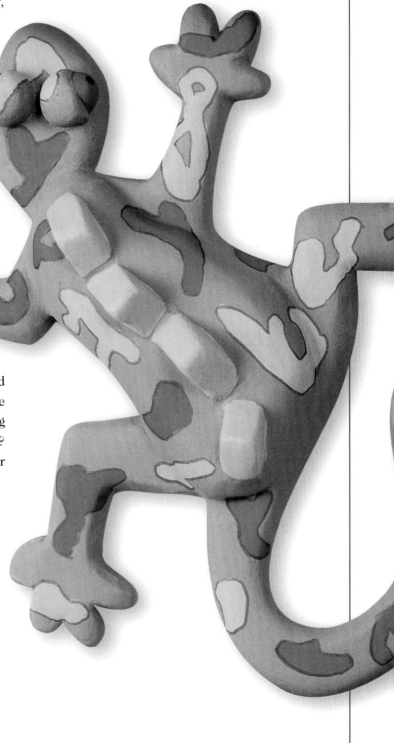

Chapter 1

Design
Basics

Start here to learn everything you need to know about sculpting foam treasures for your home.

Just having this book can entice the eyes and brain, but without the proper tools and supplies, hands can't begin to experience the fun.

Listed below are the products, techniques, and tools needed to create these pieces. Some tips and thoughts will be found only in this section, not in the individual instructions. Brand recommendations will be listed for some supplies and tools. These are the main products I use to create the projects and they have proven to work well. You can find more information on supplies in the back of the book under "Sources."

A large cutting mat is recommended for all steps. It protects the worktable, supplies a cutting base, and makes measuring very handy.

Foam

Foam is the perfect base for creating. Easily shape it by cutting, sanding, compressing—and you can attach additional shapes. Shaping is the start of all projects. Once the cover is put on the foam, the shape is difficult to change. Take your time in the beginning stages of the project, and the final outcome will be great.

The same features that make foam easy to shape, however, also make it easy to mis-shape. Store foam where it won't be bumped or broken. Suggest to those playful ones in your household that foam doesn't have a hidden desire to be used as a projectile!

I recommend STYROFOAM® brand foam for all the projects. This crisp, firm foam can be shaped easily without falling apart. Using lower-quality foam can turn a fun creation into a frustrating experience.

Patterns

Before most shaping begins, pattern or cut lines are marked. To create paper patterns, either copy the desired pattern on a copier, enlarging if necessary, or trace it from the book. Cut out the pattern and place it on the foam. Trace around the pattern with a black permanent marker. If there are internal pieces on the pattern, trace and cut the main pattern first, then you can cut and trace the internal pieces on to the foam. See photo 1.

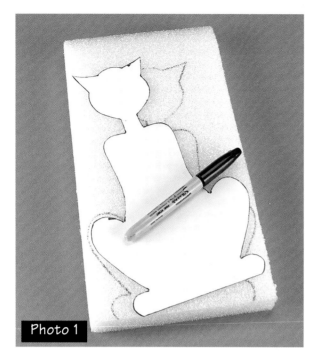

Photo 1

You can use transfer paper, but it can be difficult to see the lines. Place transfer paper face down on the foam. Place the pattern on top and go over pattern lines with a ball stylus or a dull pencil. Go back and forth a few times until a clear line can be seen on the foam. See photo 2

Photo 2

Since tracing is the easiest for most of the projects, most of the instructions will list a scissors and black marker for this method. A few of the projects have delicate details or lots of internal patterns. For these projects, transfer paper is the best route and it will be listed, along with a ball stylus, in the instructions.

There is a third way to transfer internal patterns: If the project calls for grooving the lines, set the pattern over the foam. Use a ball stylus, or the

ball end of a clay tool, to press on the pattern, lightly indenting the foam below. Remove the pattern and follow directions to press the grooves deeper. See photo 3.

Photo 3

At times, cutting lines are measured and marked directly on the foam. Follow the instructions to measure and mark rectangles, squares, and lines directly on the foam using a sharp pencil or a black permanent marker (preferred).

For eggs and balls, measuring from the top or bottom can be difficult. To make it easier, mark a dot in the top center. Start at the dot to measure down the sides, all around the form, creating a dotted line. See photo 4.

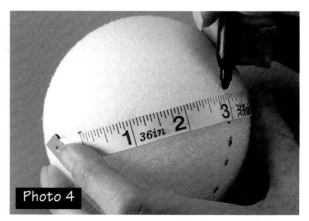

Photo 4

Create discs directly on the foam; you'll use a compass to draw the circle. The pencil side indents the foam, marking the line for cutting. When gluing the disc to the form, place the center hole that the compass created against the form to hide it.

Cutting

Rubber bands aid in marking cut lines on shapes (balls, eggs, and cones). Place a rubber band around the shape. Measure to make sure the right edge of the band is centered or at the measurement indicated in the instructions. If directed, place more rubber bands around the shape. Run a marker or sharp pencil along the right edge of the rubber band(s). Remove the rubber band(s) before cutting.

Three types of knives make different cuts easier. Use a serrated (bread or steak) knife to slice through balls, eggs, and cones; you can also use it to make long, straight cuts in 1" foam. A small craft knife (X-Acto® style) is used for cutting curves and short lines, ½" foam, and to create holes.

The third type of knife can be considered a luxury: A hot knife cuts delicate curves smoothly

Cutting Tips:

● Always use a cutting mat, or otherwise protect the surface when cutting.

● Unless otherwise noted, cuts should be made with the blade straight. Do not slant it left to right or top to bottom.

● Wax can be rubbed on the serrated or craft knife blade (not a hot knife) to make cutting easier and smoother.

● There are two options for cutting through 1" foam with a small craft knife. When the blade is put into the knife, it normally isn't long enough to cut through 1" foam without the dome (which holds the blade) indenting the foam. One option is not to insert the blade all the way in to the knife. The second option is to cut through the foam as far as the knife reaches. Using light thumb pressure, bend the foam back away from the cut line, until it snaps apart. For detailed pieces, cut a line from the pattern cut line to the outside of the foam. This will allow small pieces to be snapped off one at a time. Use an up-and-down sawing motion when cutting 1" foam.

● When making parallel cuts, it is best to cut off less foam than instructed. Then, if the cut comes out crooked, there is extra foam to cut or sand to make it parallel. A small level checks parallel cuts.

● When cutting a large ball or egg, use a serrated knife. Working over the top of the shape, cut along the line. Don't try to cut through the ball, just make a shallow cut. Turn the cut toward the table, and cut again. The first cut and the line will be the guide. Continue turning and cutting, deeper each time, until the cuts meet in the center.

and quickly. It may spoil you, though, turning a luxury into a necessity. Where a hot knife would be considerably easier, it is listed under Tools in the instructions. If you are considering purchasing a hot knife, a combination tool is very handy for all types of crafting. See Hot Tool, below, for more information.

Hot Tool

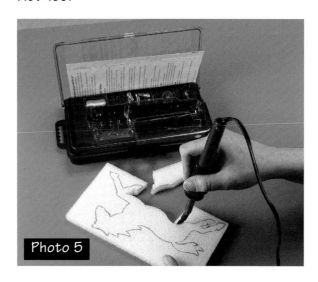

Photo 5

"Hot tool" is the generic term for a tool with various tips that get hot. The Creative Versa-Tool™ from Walnut Hollow was used for all hot knife projects; it is a small craft knife that gets very hot. The addition of heat makes cutting curves and small pieces a smooth and easy process. See photo 5. Additional tips are included with the tool making it very versatile for crafting. The Flow Point works well for creating grooves. Instructions call for it when creating the Large Carved Pedestal.

Foam-sanding

Sanding rounds edges, creates grooves, and shapes. A scrap piece of foam is rubbed against the foam shape. Flat sides of scraps are used to round edges. Grooves are created with edges or points. And the curves left from cutting out circles are great for sanding curved edges or making discs symmetrical. See photo 6.

Photo 6

Scraps can be cut to any size to make sanding easier. See photo 7.

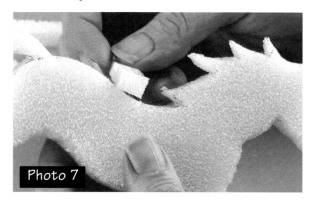

Photo 7

When the instructions state to "slightly round" the edges, very little sanding is needed. Sand just enough to take the point off the edge—finger pressing works for this also. See far left example in photo 8.

HOT TOOL TIPS:

● Work in a well-ventilated area. The tool works by melting the foam, thus producing fumes.

● Practice on scrap pieces first.

● Don't hold the tip in one area, keep it moving.

● When indenting the foam, the tool doesn't need to touch the foam. Hold the tool above the foam, lowering it until the foam begins to melt. The foam will get hot and will keep melting a few seconds after the tool is removed.

● Melted foam is very difficult to sand. Try picking off the hard foam first, then sand.

For rounded edges, sand a bit more for a soft, round edge. See photo 8, center example. More sanding is needed to slope the edge. There should be a smooth curve from the side to the top. See far right example in photo 8.

Photo 8

Compressing

Compressing foam is done to round edges, create grooves and indentations, and flatten the foam. Fingers are the best tools to use when compressing edges to lightly round them. Simply rub the foam and gently press.

When listed in the instructions, finger pressing is used to smooth and clean the foam. Use a finger to rub along the foam to smooth and compact it and also remove loose pieces of foam. This is a great clean-up step to use before the foam is covered.

For creating grooves, indentations, and flattening the foam, clay tools can be used. The ball end is the choice tool for creating wide grooves. Press gently on the foam to create a groove. If a deeper groove is needed, make another pass with the tool. See photo 9. Pressing too deeply on the first pass will rip the foam.

Photo 9

Sometimes the instructions will call for the curved end of a clay tool. This tool is great for indentations and grooves that have at least one straight up and down side. The wide end of a knife works well for compressing large areas.

Gluing

Photo 10

To join foam pieces, apply a dab or line of glue to one of the pieces. Press the pieces together lightly. Rub or twist the pieces to spread the glue, then press firmly. Set aside to dry. Glue created for use with foam is recommended. Projects in this book use Hold the Foam™ from Beacon™ Adhesives. It works well and holds fast. The glue will hold in about 45 minutes, and will be totally dry in 24 hours.

Toothpicks are sometimes a necessity for joining pieces. If this is the case, they will be in the supply list and instructions. See photo 10. A level is listed as a tool when pedestals and candleholders are glued together. This is to ensure that the glued and stacked pieces don't lean.

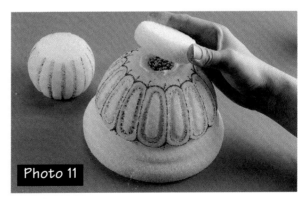

Photo 11

BB Weights

BBs are used to add weight. Weight, of course, doesn't alter the final look of the piece, but keeps it from blowing over, and gives your project a substantial heft. See photo 11.

Follow the instructions for the size and depth of the hole. It is easiest to use a small craft knife to cut around the hole. Then use the blade or clay tool to pick the foam out of the center of the hole. Repeat until the hole is the recommended depth. Pour the BBs into the hole. Press down on them to make sure they are packed together, adding more if necessary. Packing them will prevent rattling when the creation is picked up. Apply glue around the hole and follow the instructions to add the foam piece that covers the hole.

Clean Up

Before moving on to the next step in creating—covering the foam—make sure to clean up. Tap project to remove any loose particles. Finger pressing also works well for this. Clean particles from work area. This will keep foam particles from mixing with the covering.

Paperclay

The feel of Creative Paperclay ® is unique. It contains volcanic ash and wood pulp, not earthen clay. It is easy to work with, air hardens, and is clean and odorless. You'll use it not only to cover the foam, but to add clay shapes to further develop the form of the creation.

Tip: Nail marks and indentations from rings can be annoying when working with the clay. Remember to take off jewelry and, unless you use regular tools more often than your fingers, short-trimmed nails are suggested.

Tools

When "clay supplies" appears in the supply list, you'll need the following items. You'll find it helpful to put these items in containers to grab easily when needed. Some of the items may already be listed in the instructions for shaping the foam.

- **Wax paper or plastic**
- **Water**
- **Wood clay tools**
- **Art brushes**
- **Small craft knife**
- **Rolling pin**

The first thing you will need is a work surface. Paperclay has a great capacity for sticking. To prevent this, use wax paper or plastic (a garbage bag) to cover the work area.

To smooth the clay, keep handy a small bowl of water. It need only be big enough to dip small bits of clay into, or to wet fingers. For wetting large areas and keeping the entire project damp, use a fine-mist spray bottle filled with water.

Clay tools come in all shapes and sizes. They help to smooth clay in areas that fingers can't reach. I prefer wood tools. They work well with paperclay and for shaping the foam. See the picture under foam compressing (page 11).

A small art brush, #8 flat, can help to smooth hard-to-reach areas. Dampen and brush it along the clay to smooth.

In most cases, you'll need a small craft knife to shape the foam. This knife is also used to cut clay shapes.

I use whatever is handy as a rolling pin. I find the heel of my hand to be the handiest when flattening clay for small pieces. Use acrylic paint bottles, round pencils, or scrap pieces of wood dowel to roll out the clay. Cover the clay with additional wax paper or plastic to prevent it from sticking to the roller.

Patterns

To transfer patterns onto clay, a paper pattern is needed. Cut the pattern out. Place it on the flattened clay and trace around it. Use a small craft knife to trace on, as well as cut through the clay.

Covering Foam

Pinch off a bit of clay. Place it against the foam. Use your thumb to press it into and across the surface of the ball. The result will be a very thin layer of clay. See photo 12. Continue to cover the foam according to the instructions. Fingers dipped in water will help smooth the clay. Clay tools help to smooth clay between attached pieces and in hard-to-reach areas.

All the clay projects have a handmade charm. The clay doesn't need to be absolutely smooth, but there should be a uniform shape—no lumps and valleys unless instructions call for them.

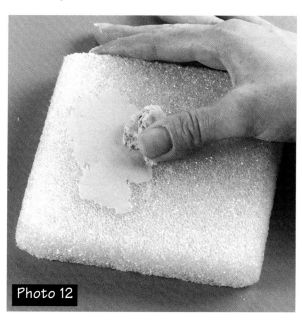
Photo 12

The process of covering the foam can be stopped at any time. Paperclay will stick to itself when the dry clay is moistened with a bit of water. In fact, the clay will stick to most things when the surface is dampened.

Adding Clay Pieces

Cut the pattern out from clay or form the instructed shape. If the instructions call for it, smooth the edges. Rub a damp finger against the clay to smooth any jagged edges. See photo 13.

Photo 13

Next, dip the side to be attached lightly in water. Water can also be applied by dipping a finger in water and rubbing along the clay. Press in place. The instructions will state to place the shape on or press it against the main form.

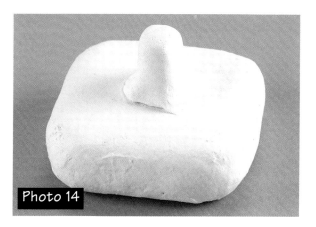
Photo 14

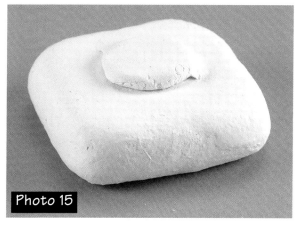
Photo 15

Pressing or pushing the clay piece to the form causes the clay to buckle up next to the form. Smooth this excess clay to the main form. See photo 14. When the clay piece is set on the form, the clay is smoothed from the edges of the pieces. The result is an attached piece that is smaller than the original pattern. See photo 15. Fingers, clay tools, and brushes dipped in water all can be used to smooth the clay.

Drying

Room temperature, humidity, and clay thickness will affect the drying time of the clay. It is recommended to let it dry for at least 24 hours. It dries from the outside in, making it sometimes difficult to judge its dryness. It is better to be patient than to rush the project.

If dry clay is cracked, fill in the crack with fresh clay and allow it to dry before sanding.

Sanding Clay

Sanding is mainly done to remove imperfections such as finger or nail prints. It also softens the look of the piece. None of the projects using paperclay are meant to be porcelain smooth. The style is more rustic or primitive.

Sanding is done with a quarter sheet of 220 grit sandpaper, which you can rip or fold into any size or shape to make sanding easier. To remove the dust after sanding, wipe with a damp cloth.

Storage

To keep the clay moist, wrap it tightly in plastic wrap and then place it in an airtight storage bag. If the clay begins to dry out, mist it with water, close the bag, and allow the clay to absorb the water. Or, knead a few drops of water into the clay to restore its pliability.

Joint Compound

Joint compound can be found in most home centers. I used Plus 3™ Sheetrock® Lightweight All Purpose Joint Compound on all the projects. The important attribute of this compound is that it won't shrink or crack. See photo 16.

It is important to have the form exactly as needed before covering with compound. Joint compound can't be used to fill large gaps or correct a form. If needed, paperclay can be used to fill in or fix areas. When clay has dried, the compound can be applied.

To create different looks, the only tools you'll need are a 1" art brush and sandpaper. To begin, scoop out a small amount of compound with a 1" art brush. Place the compound on the form, and brush it against the foam. See photo 17.

Photo 16

Photo 17

Photo 18

Brush on the compound. Brush back and forth, working into the foam surface. It will look bumpy when done. See photo 18.

For a slightly rustic look, sand the compound lightly. Sand just enough to smooth roughness and expose any air pockets. Foam showing in an area ¼" or larger will need to be re-coated, allowed to dry, and sanded. See photo 19.

To get an ultra-smooth look, after sanding apply another coat of compound. Brush back and forth across the form to fill in any air pockets or gaps. Dipping the brush lightly in water will help to smooth on the compound.

When totally dry, the project is sanded smooth with ultra-fine sandpaper. The process can be repeated until the piece is as smooth as desired. Sanding between multiple applications is the key to a smooth finish. See photo 19.

Photo 19

For a more rustic look, brush the compound back and forth, covering the foam well. Add more compound over the top, this time roughly. The rougher the compound is when applied, the more pitted and rustic the outcome. If the compound is brushed too much, it will become smooth. To roughen it again, let the compound dry a few minutes. Swipe the compound roughly with the brush. When the compound is dry, lightly sand. Sand only enough to smooth the highest parts. See photo 20.

Photo 20

Sanding is not necessary for a textured finish. Brush one coat of thick compound. Cover as much foam as possible. Small spots of uncovered foam won't ruin this look. Here again, if the compound is brushed too much, it will become smooth. To roughen it again, let the compound dry a few minutes. Swipe the compound roughly with the brush. See photo 21.

Photo 21

Sanding Joint Compound

Sanding produces lots of fine dust; avoid breathing it. Clean up immediately with a shop vacuum. Follow by wiping with a damp cloth or paper towel. Working over a towel will trap the dust, keeping it from spreading over the work area.

Sanding is done with a quarter sheet folded or ripped into convenient shapes and sizes. Most sanding is done with 220 grit sandpaper. For an ultra smooth look, do the final sanding with 400 grit sandpaper.

TIPS:

● Spackling (used to patch wall holes) can be used to fill in small holes after the second sanding.

● Joint compound doesn't work well as a gap filler. Use paperclay instead to fill in a gap. When the clay has dried it can be covered with a thin layer of compound.

Drying

The first coat of compound will take 12-24 hours to dry. Additional coats take less time. Oven drying is not recommended. While the compound isn't listed as non-toxic, avoid breathing the fumes. Project can be put in front of a heating vent to speed drying.

Painting

While the foam shape and the covering used give the creation form and texture, paint adds life. It is used to add color, highlight the texture and define details. Few tools are needed, brushes being the most important. The acrylic paint used in all the projects is Americana® from DecoArt™.

Tools for Painting

The quality and size of brushes make a big difference to the outcome of the projects. These brushes are necessities: 1", ½", #8 flat, a #4 or #5 round, and a small liner. The 1" and ½" brushes are for applying a base coat, dry brush, or color wash. The flat or round brushes also are used to apply the base coat, but in tighter areas. A round brush can also be used to add detail, and the liner is for fine detail.

The smaller the area being painted (the smaller the brush), the more important the quality and condition of the brush. Purchase middle-of-the-line brushes. The cheaper ones don't last as well, and top-of-the-line brushes need a huge commitment to take care of them while using them and cleaning them to justify the price. Foam brushes won't do what bristle brushes do—don't substitute.

To keep brushes in good condition, always wash them well. After rinsing excess paint out with water, brush bristles back and forth in soap until suds appear. It is surprising how much more paint comes out of the brush. Don't use soap with oils; use dish soap or an Ivory™ bar. Follow with final water rinse. Never allow paint to dry on the brush or the brush to sit in water for too long.

Besides brushes, a paint pallet, water container, and paper towels are needed. Convenience is more important than quality. A paper plate can be used as a paint pallet and a plastic disposable cup to hold water.

Base Coat

When instructions state "paint," a good, solid coat of paint is needed. For the best results, you will usually need to apply two coats of paint. Some paint colors tend to be translucent. For these colors, add a bit of black or white to the paint. Apply a solid coverage with the mixture and follow with a coat of the original paint.

Dry Brushing

This technique is used to highlight texture or to make the creation look old. Very little paint is used for each layer. A 1" or ½" brush is used most often, but a #8 flat can be used to dry brush smaller areas. Dry brushing and painting textured pieces can be rough on a brush; use old brushes for these techniques when possible.

To dry brush, rinse brush in water to remove any leftover soap. Blot brush on paper towel until brush is just damp. Load a little paint onto the brush. In a clean area of the pallet, gently stroke the brush back and forth, working the paint up into the bristles. Wipe brush gently on paper towel to remove excess paint. Using just the tip of the brush, lightly brush color randomly across the creation. The paint will cover only the highest areas.

Photo 20

Photo 20

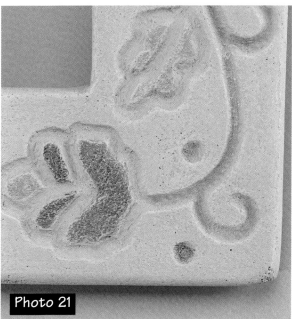

Photo 21

The result should be uniform. If there are blotches or a line where the brush first touches the project, wipe off more paint from the brush onto paper towel. Make sure the brush is just barely damp when starting. If the brush needs to be reloaded frequently, try stroking the brush back and forth on the pallet more. This will work the majority of the paint up the bristles so less needs to be wiped off. Also, try rinsing the brush and starting over with a clean, barely-damp brush. When dry brushing for a while, the paint begins to accumulate and dry on the brush, causing the need to reload often.

Instructions often will call for you to dry brush many colors on the surface. This is usually done with transparent paint to build layers of color, adding a lot of depth to the project. Allow each layer to dry (it won't take long) before moving to the next color. When applying the paint in a random fashion, some of the dry brushing will show in its original color, while in other areas, the color will be changed by a dry brush of another color over the top of it.

Another reason for multiple colors is to create a lighter base so a transparent color can be seen.

For example, when the project starts out with Lamp Black, Bronze highlights can barely be seen. By dry brushing a lighter, opaque color first, the Bronze shows better.

With both dry brushing and washing, adding more layers is better. Repeat any or all layers until you're happy with the results.

Wash

Washing adds a transparent color over the top. Unlike dry brushing, which highlights only the highest areas, color washing covers the entire surface. It changes the original color. It can add shading and highlight the texture of the creation.

To create transparent color, water is mixed in with the paint—how much depends on the paint. Some colors are already translucent and only a drop is needed. Others are opaque and need a bit more. Always add just a few drops at a time and test the color on a piece of paper towel; it should look like a water color.

A 1" brush is used to wash the color on. Smaller brushes can be used for smaller areas.

Photo 22

Load the brush as normal (the paint shouldn't be dripping off), and stroke it on. See photo 22. Sometimes, the instructions will ask you to blot the paint with a paper towel to lighten the effect and soften any brush lines.

Dry Brush with Wash

To use this technique, mix the paint to a watercolor consistency like a color wash, but load the brush and apply paint using the dry brush technique. Turning the paint into a wash makes it more transparent.

Protective Finishes

None of the projects are shown with a protective finish. Nor do the instructions call for one. But it is worth considering. Use a brush or spray finish in matt, semi-gloss, or gloss. Besides protecting the piece, a protective finish will brighten the colors.

Chapter 2

Double Duty

Sometimes, art has a hint of function —plaques fill blank walls and sculptures hold down shelves and counter tops! The projects in this chapter are truly functional. They can hold candles, display pictures, or tell you the time.

Cone Candle Pedestals

Skill level: Easy

Three foam discs and a cone were used to create each of the candle pedestals. The key is to cut the cones so the tops and bottoms are parallel. Careful measurements and sanding will help with this.

SUPPLIES

Foam:
  9" cone
  ½" sheet, 12" x 12"
Paperclay
Foam glue
Acrylic paint:
  Antique White
  Raw Sienna
  Light Cinnamon
  Forest Green
BBs

TOOLS

Ruler
Measuring tape
Rubber band
Compass
Black marker
Small craft knife
Small level
Clay supplies
Sandpaper: 220 grit

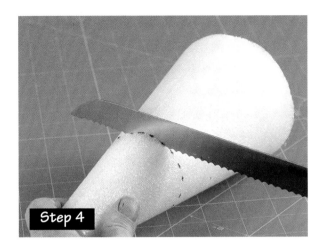

Step 4

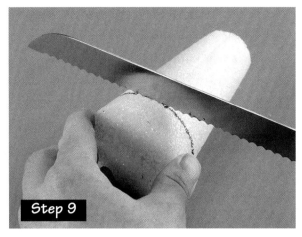

Step 9

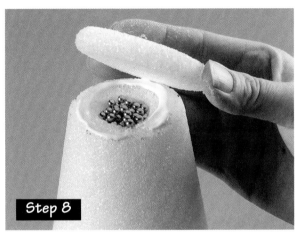

Step 8

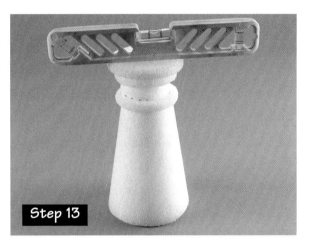

Step 13

Instructions

1. Cut two 3" and one 3⅝" disc from the ½" foam sheet.

2. Foam-sand around the outside edge of discs, making them symmetrical. Foam-sand to round the top and bottom edges.

3. Apply glue to back of the 3" disc. Press against the 3⅝" disc, centered. Set these discs and second 3" disc aside.

4. Place marks around cone 5¼" from bottom. Connect marks to form line. Cut cone along line. Set top of cone aside.

5. Make sure the top cut is parallel to the bottom of the cone. If necessary, sand the top to make parallel.

6. Create a 1"-wide, 2"-deep hole in the center of the cone's top.

7. Pack hole tightly with BBs.

8. Apply glue around the hole. Press a 3" disc against it, centered. Set aside.

9. Place marks around the top cone section 5/8" from bottom. Connect marks to form a line. Cut along the line. Save the bottom section and discard the top section.

10. Make sure the top and bottom of the small cone piece are parallel. If necessary, sand to make parallel.

11. Apply glue to the bottom, wider end of the small cone section. Press on top 3" disc and large cone section, centering.

12. Apply glue to top of small cone section. Press discs from step 3 on top; centered with 3" disc against cone.

13. Check to make sure pedestal is level. Place weight (candle) on pedestal and set aside until glue is completely dry.

14. Cover the pedestal with clay. Allow to dry.

15. Sand any rough areas or flaws. Wipe off dust.

16. Paint bottom section with Antique White.

17. Paint bottom and top circle with Forest Green.

18. Paint the rest of the pedestal Light Cinnamon.

19. Wash Raw Sienna over the pedestal. Use a wadded piece of paper towel to blot and rub paint, softening paint edges. When dry, repeat with second Raw Sienna wash.

Frame Hanging Options

There is one must-do, and two options for the frames in this chapter. Wire loops must be created to hold the acrylic sheet, photo, and frame back in place. An easel is an option for a self-standing frame. To hang the frame on a wall, use a Wall Hanger (see below).

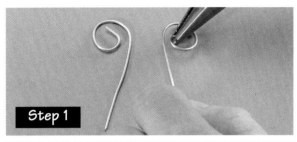

Step 1

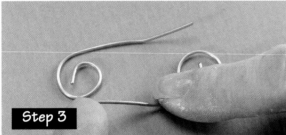

Step 3

Step 4

Wire Loops

SUPPLIES

7" of 16 gauge wire
Wire cutter
Needle nose pliers

Instructions

1. Cut 3½" wire. Using the picture as a guide, form one end into ⅝" wide loop.

2. Lay the loop on a work surface with the long, straight end to right. Place a finger on the wire ¾" from the straight end. Bend the straight end up until it sticks ¼" above the work surface.

3. Repeat with the second wire.

4. Follow frame instructions for loop location. Push loop's straight end into the side of frame opening with loop straight up (perpendicular to frame back). Insert until bend is flush with side of frame.

5. Turn the loop to sit flush against the back of the frame.

Wall Hanger Option

Use this simple hanger to hang plaques or frames on the wall.

SUPPLIES

18 gauge wire, 2"
Wire cutter
Needle nose pliers
Pencil

Instructions

1. ⅞" from one end, bend wire at 90 degree (right) angle.

2. ¼" from bend, make another 90 degree bend to create "U."

3. Bend bottom ⅜" of "U" up at 45 degree angle.

4. Insert hanger into back of creation, prongs toward the top and at a slight angle.

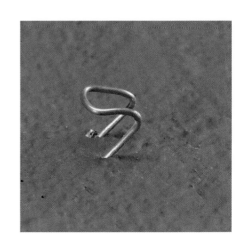

Easel Option

This option is for two-piece frames.

SUPPLIES

14 gauge wire
Wire cutter
Needle nose pliers

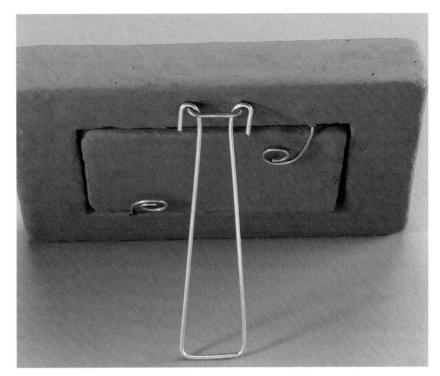

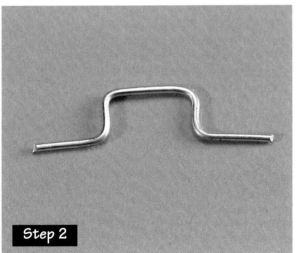
Step 2

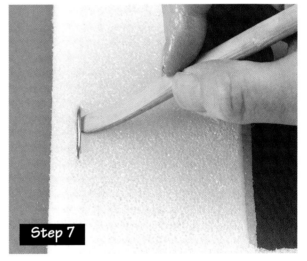
Step 7

Instructions for Wire Bar

Note: The wire bar needs to be inserted into the foam before you are instructed to glue the two frames together.

1. Cut 3" of wire. Mark 1" from each end. At marks, bend the wire up at 90 degree (right) angle to create "U."

2. Place a mark ½" up from bottom on each side of "U." At marks, bend wire out at 90 degree angle to give "U" wings.

3. Draw 1" line on second (narrower) frame ½" from top and centered left to right.

4. Cut through foam along line.

5. Insert the wire bar through the cut, bottom of "U" sticking out from back of frame. Wings will be against foam to be glued to front frame piece.

6. Pull on bottom of "U" until the wings sink into the foam, just below surface, and the bottom of the "U" sticks out ⅛".

7. Compress foam the ½" above, ½" below, and under the wire bar.

8. Continue with the remaining frame instructions.

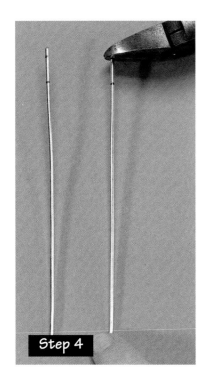

Step 4

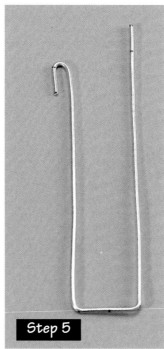

Step 5

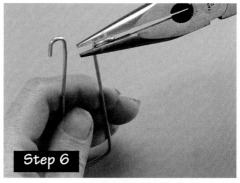

Step 6

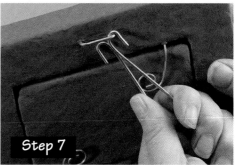

Step 7

Instructions for Wire Easel

1. Measure the distance from the wire bar to the frame bottom then multiply by two and add 2". Cut the wire to this measurement.

2. Find center, mark ½" to each side. At marks, bend wire up at 90 degree (right) angle to create "U." Make sure the sides of the "U" are parallel and the bottom of the "U" is straight.

3. Place mark up from bottom on each side of "U." The distance is the same as the distance from the wire bar to the frame bottom.

4. Place mark ½" above each mark. Cut off any excess wire above ½" marks.

5. At marks, bend wire down into loop, wire ends pointing down to bottom of the "U." The tops of the loops should be the same distance from the "U" bottom.

6. Put pliers over both sides of the loop, and bend the loop forward slightly. Repeat on the second loop. The more the wire is bent, the more angled back the frame will sit.

7. Insert one loop under the wire bar on the back of the frame. Squeeze wire easel sides together until the second loop can be placed under the wire bar.

8. Release the sides of the wire easel and pull down. Each wire loop should wrap around the sides of the wire bar.

Floral Frame

Skill level: Easy

This a simple project to create. The foam is grooved to create the pattern, and the joint compound creates the texture. Only a light sanding and minimal paint skills are needed.

SUPPLIES

½" foam sheet, 12" x 20"
Joint compound
Foam glue
Acrylic paints:
   Fawn
   Deep Midnight Blue
   Gingerbread
   Rookwood Red
   Light Avocado
   Antique White
3⅞" x 5⅞" acrylic glazing
   sheet*
Transfer paper
2 wire loops
Paper pattern
<u>Optional:</u> Wall Hanger or
   Easel Back

TOOLS

Ruler
Black marker
Ball clay tool
Utility knife
Rolling pin
Sandpaper: 220 grit
Ball stylus

* These sheets come larger than needed. Instructions are included for cutting the sheet.

Instructions

1. Cut two 10" x 12" foam rectangles.

2. Mark a line on one frame 3¼" in from all sides to create 3½" x 5½" rectangle in the center. Cut out the rectangle. This rectangle can be used for sanding later.

3. Mark a line on the second frame 3" in from all sides to create a 4" x 6" rectangle in the center. Cut out the rectangle. Set the center rectangle aside for use later. *Optional:* If using the easel

option, insert the wire bar before the next step.

4. Apply glue on the second (narrower) frame around the picture opening and outer edge. Press the two frames together. Make sure the outer edges line up. Set the frame under weights (books) for 45 minutes.

5. Remove weights, foam-sand the edges to make sure they are plumb and square. Round the edges and corners. Don't round the edge on picture opening in back.

Step 6

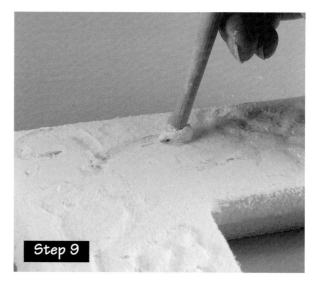

Step 9

Step 7

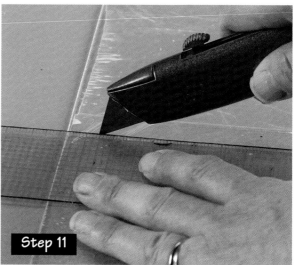

Step 11

6. Place the pattern on the frame and transfer inside the lines. Either press on the pattern with a ball clay tool, indenting foam, or use transfer paper and a ball stylus. Press ⅛" deep grooves along pattern lines. Note: Grooves will be wider than pattern lines.

7. To make the back cover, use a rolling pin to compress the 4" x 6" foam rectangle to ¼" depth. Trim by ⅛" to 3⅞" x 5⅞".

Optional: If using the easel option, compress the foam ½" above, ½" below and under wire bar before the next step.

8. Spread on a layer of joint compound. Coat the face, edges of the opening, and two side edges. Brush back and forth and in a swirling motion to push the compound into foam crevices. Make sure to cover foam well.

9. Use the ball clay tool to remove excess compound in grooves. Run tool through the grooves, frequently wiping the ball clean. Brush down the ridges that form on groove edges.

10. Brush compound on two side edges and face of back cover. When dry, coat rest of frame and back cover. Set aside to dry.

11. Cut 3⅞" x 5⅞" acrylic glazing sheet. Mark line for cutting width. Using ruler as guide, make repeated cuts with utility knife to deeply score acrylic. Turn acrylic over to backside. Using light thumb pressure, bend acrylic back, away from score line, until it snaps apart. Repeat to cut length. Set aside.

12. Very lightly sand frame and back cover. Sand only to smooth bumps. To smooth grooves, go over with ball tool, gently applying pressure.

13. Sand smooth edges that acrylic glazing sheet will set against. Wipe off dust.

14. Paint frame and cover Fawn. Adding a bit of water to paint will help to fill in grooves and holes.

15. With dry brush, paint in colors, using the picture as guide. Keep brush dry and wipe across frame's surface. Don't fill in holes with paint.

16. Dry brush Antique White, covering top surface and indented berries.

17. Set frame face down. Place glazing sheet in frame. Place picture on top. Place back cover on top.

18. Insert wire loop into left side of frame, 1½" from top.

19. Repeat to insert second loop on right side, 1½" from bottom.

Floral Frame pattern
Enlarge to 200%

Horse Frame

Skill level: Easy

SUPPLIES

½" foam sheet, 12" x 12"
Black crepe paper
Decoupage medium
Joint compound
Foam glue
Thick white glue
Acrylic paints:
    Lamp Black
    Burnt Sienna
    Raw Sienna
    Fawn
    Dark Chocolate
3⅞" x 5⅞" acrylic glazing
    sheet*
2 wire loops
Paper pattern
<u>*Optional:*</u> Wall Hanger or
    Easel Back

TOOLS

Ruler
Black marker
Hot knife
Utility knife
Rolling pin
Sandpaper: 220 grit
Small plastic container
Water

* These sheets come larger than
needed. Instructions are included
for cutting the sheet.

A horse in full gallop is a beauty for all ages. The horse and frame were created separately. Once the frame was decoupaged, I attached the horse. This makes changing the looks of the frame easy. First follow the instructions to create the foam frame and horse. Then cover the frame with paperclay or joint compound. Finally attach the horse to the frame. The horse is delicate to cut, coat, and sand, but the project as a whole is easy.

Instructions

1. Cut two 9" x 11" foam rectangles.

2. Mark line on one frame 2¾" in from all sides to create 3½" x 5½" rectangle in center. Cut out rectangle. This rectangle can be used for sanding later.

3. Mark line on second frame 2½" in from all sides to create 4" x 6" rectangle in center. Cut out rectangle. Set center rectangle aside for use later.

Optional: If using Easel Option, insert wire bar before next step.

4. Apply glue on the second (narrower) frame around picture opening and outer edge. Press two frames together. Make sure outer edges line up.

5. Cut 5¼", 6", and 4" long by ½" wide foam strips. Use rolling pin to compress foam strips to ¼" depth. Foam-sand to round edges.

6. Glue strips to front of frame, ¾" from inside opening, 5¼" on left, 8" on top, and 4" on right side. There is ½" space between bottom of 8" piece and top of side pieces. Set frame under weights (books) for 45 minutes.

7. Remove weights, foam-sand edges to make sure they are plumb and square. Round edges and corners. Don't round edge on picture opening in back.

8. Use rolling pin to compress 4" x 6" foam rectangle to ¼" depth. Trim rectangle by ⅛" to 3⅞" x 5⅞". This is the back cover.

Optional: If using Easel Option, compress foam ½" above, ½" below, and under wire bar before next step.

Step 8

9. Rip crepe paper into irregular-shaped pieces, 1" or smaller. Brush 1" area of decoupage medium on frame. Lay crepe paper on medium and brush with second coat of medium. Brush on more laminate, some over attached crepe paper and some on foam. Lay crepe paper on laminate and brush with second coat. Continue adding crepe paper until frame and back cover are covered. Set aside until completely dry; the crepe paper will look cloudy.

Step 9

10. Cut the horse pattern (page 30), and trace onto foam. Cut out. Foam-sand to round edges.

11. Mix ¼ cup joint compound with 1 tablespoon water until smooth. Brush a layer over horse. Brush back and forth to work mixture into gaps and air bubble holes. As compound seeps into horse, apply another coat. Allow to dry.

12. Gently sand horse. If desired, apply more diluted compound to cover air holes.

13. Paint frame, back cover, and horse Lamp Black.

14. Dry brush decoupage areas with Burnt Sienna, then Raw Sienna, and finally Fawn.

15. Wash Dark Chocolate over frame.

16. Attach horse to frame with thick white glue, using picture as guide.

17. Cut 3⅞" x 5⅞" piece from acrylic glazing sheet. Mark line for cutting width. Using ruler as guide, make repeated cuts to deeply score acrylic. Turn acrylic over to backside. Using light thumb pressure, bend the acrylic back, away from the score line, until it snaps apart. Repeat to cut length.

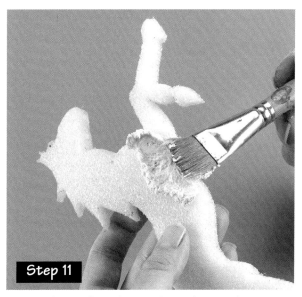
Step 11

18. Set frame face down. Place glazing sheet in frame. Place picture on top. Place back cover on top.

19. Insert wire loop into left side of frame, 1" from top.

20. Repeat to insert second loop on right side, 1" from bottom.

Horse Frame pattern

Pine Cone Frame

Skill level: Medium

The pine cones for this simple and rustic frame were created by flattening clay balls into discs, then pressing them to the frame. No need to stop with two cones. Keep up the fun and sprinkle the cones all around the frame.

SUPPLIES

½" foam sheet 12" x 7"
Paperclay
Foam glue
Acrylic paints:
    Terra Cotta
    Light Cinnamon
    Lamp Black
3⅞" x 5⅞" acrylic glazing
    sheet*
2 wire loops
<u>Optional:</u> Wall Hanger or
    Easel Back

TOOLS

Ruler
Black marker
Rolling pin
Clay supplies
Sandpaper: 220 grit
Utility knife
Small craft knife

* These sheets come larger than needed. Instructions are included for cutting the sheet.

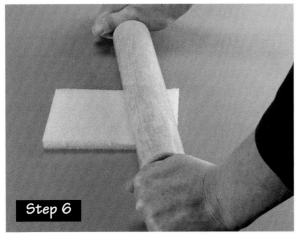

Step 6

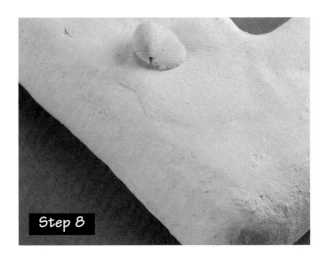

Step 8

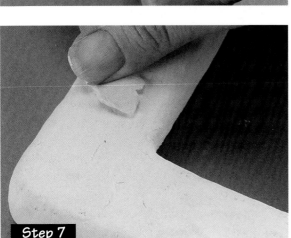

Step 7

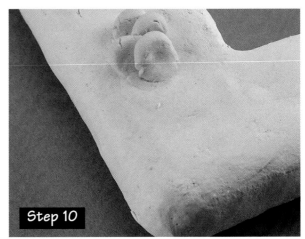

Step 10

Instructions

1. Cut two 7" x 5½" foam rectangles.

2. Mark line on one frame 1½" in from all sides to create 4" x 2½" rectangle in center. Cut out rectangle. This rectangle can be used for sanding later.

3. Mark a line on the second frame 1¼" in from all sides to create a 4½" x 3" rectangle in center. Cut out rectangle. Set center rectangle aside for use later.

Optional: If using Easel Option, insert wire bar before next step.

4. Apply glue on second (narrower) frame around picture opening and outer edge. Press two frames together. Make sure outer edges line up, then set frame under weights (books) for 45 minutes.

5. Remove weights; foam-sand edges to make sure plumb and square. Foam-sand to round corners and edges. Don't round edge on picture opening in back.

6. To create the back cover, use a rolling pin to compress 4½" x 3" foam rectangle to ¼" depth. Trim rectangle by ⅛" to 4⅜" x 2⅞".

Optional: If using Easel Option, compress foam ½" above, ½" below, and under wire bar before next step.

7. Cover frame and back cover with paperclay. Don't attempt to cover smoothly. The finish should be textured, especially on face and sides of frame. To add more texture, smooth small bits of clay flattened to ⅟₁₆". Smooth edges of blotches to frame.

8. Roll twenty ¼" to ⅜" balls for pine cone. Roll one ball into oval, flatten slightly and dip end into water. Press wet tip onto frame, 2" from bottom and centered left to right. This is the tip of the first pine cone.

9. Repeat, adding one petal to the left and one to the right of and both slightly below the first one.

10. Form fourth petal and place slightly below and centered between last two.

11. Continue adding petals using picture as guide. As cone is created, petals should become straighter up and down. For the last three rows, push petals straight down onto frame, making sure ends are dipped in water so they stick.

12. Repeat process to add second pine cone.

13. Roll 1" clay ball, then press to disc ³⁄₁₆" thick. Rub water on back of disc and press onto frame between cones, in corner. Set frame aside until dry.

14. Cut 4⅜" x 2⅞" piece from acrylic glazing sheet. Mark line for cutting width. Using ruler as guide, make repeated cuts to deeply score acrylic. Turn acrylic over to backside. Using light thumb pressure, bend acrylic back, away from score line, until it snaps apart. Repeat to cut length. Set aside.

15. Sand rough areas and flaws on frame. Wipe off dust.

16. Paint pine cones and button Lamp Black.

17. Dry brush Light Cinnamon over cones.

18. Highlight tips with dry brush of Terra Cotta.

19. Paint button inside and rest of frame Terra Cotta.

20. Set frame face down. Place glazing sheet in the frame. Place picture on top. Place back cover on top.

21. Insert wire loop into the side of the frame along the bottom and ¾" from left.

22. Repeat to insert second loop, along top and ¾" from right.

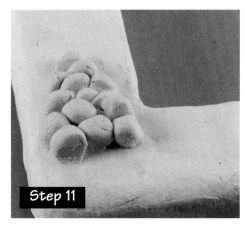

Step 11

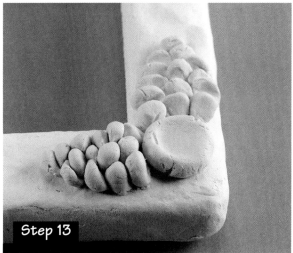

Step 13

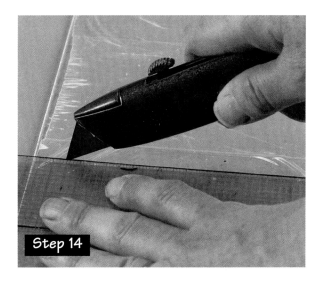

Step 14

Vase Pedestal

Skill level: Medium

With great joy and a huge pile of white foam dust, I discovered the fun of creating vase shapes with foam. This project is scaled down from the original experiments, keeping the amount of foam dust down. To enlarge the fun, add more layers. Samples of taller pedestals can be found in The Gallery.

SUPPLIES

Foam:
  1" sheet, 4" x 6"
  ½" sheet, 12" x 8"
  3" ball
Joint compound
Foam glue
Acrylic paints:
  Avocado
  Light Avocado
  Celery Green
  Raw Umber
  Raw Sienna
BBs

TOOLS

Black marker
Level
Ruler
Compass
Small craft knife
Sandpaper: 220 grit
Art brushes

Instructions

1. Cut 4" and 2" discs from 1" foam. Cut two 3" and one 3½", 2½", and 4" disc from ½" foam.

2. Cut bottom and top ¼" off 3" ball. Make sure cuts are parallel.

3. Foam-sand bottom of ball to lightly round edge.

4. Foam-sand edges of all ½"-deep discs to round.

5. Foam-sand 4" x 1" disc to round bottom edge and slope top edge. Set sanded discs aside.

6. Do not sand edges of the 2" x 1" disc. Make sure it is symmetrically round but don't round edges.

7. Place marks on sides of disc, ½" down from top, forming a dotted line. Apply glue to bottom center of disc. Place glue side against top of 3" ball. Press together.

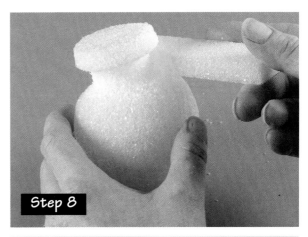

Step 8

8. While holding pieces together, sand below line with edge of ½" scrap foam. Sand ¼" deep groove around form. If keeping pieces together is difficult, set aside for 24 hours until glue is dry.

9. Sand below groove to angle out to widest area of ball.

Note: There are many pleasing vase shapes. Stop shaping when vase shape is eye pleasing and symmetrical.

10. Sand rim above groove to round edges.

11. Create hole through bottom center of vase shape, 1" wide and 1¼" deep. This will be filled with BBs later. Set aside.

12. Stack 3½" then 3" and finally 2½" disc, center.

Step 9

Step 10

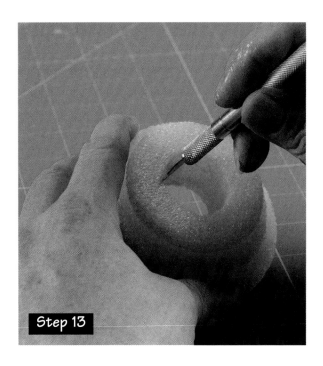

Step 13

Step 17

13. Create hole through center of discs, 1" wide. Un-stack discs. Apply glue around holes and re-stack, press firmly together. Set aside.

14. The pedestal will be assembled upside down. Set 4" x ½" disc face down, compass hole up, on work table. Glue 3" disc, centered, on top. Glue vase shape, upside down and centered, on top.

15. Glue stack of ½" discs on top, centered, with holes aligned.

16. Pack hole tightly with BBs.

17. Glue base in place, centered. Let dry 45 minutes.

18. Spread on layer of joint compound to half of pedestal. Allow to dry. Apply compound to other half. Allow to dry.

19. Sand pedestal. Don't over-sand. There will be pits and valleys, yet the pedestal should not feel rough to touch. Foam showing in an area ¼" or

larger will need to be recoated, allowed to dry and sanded.

20. Apply Avocado base coat.

21. Randomly dry brush areas of Celery Green. Keep edges of painted areas soft and rounded, not sharp and straight. Make sure to paint in-between discs.

22. Repeat with Raw Umber, overlapping colors.

23. Repeat with Raw Sienna, overlapping colors.

24. Repeat using all three colors in this order: Celery Green, Raw Umber and Raw Sienna. The paints are transparent so colors should show through from layers.

25. Dry brush wash of Light Avocado over pedestal.

Large Carved Pedestal

Skill level: Medium

This pedestal was created to accommodate a 5" candle, but it looks just as great displaying your favorite Covered Foam Creature or a potted plant. Its elegant style looks more complicated than it is. Two pieces of foam were carved and stacked with six discs. The Ultimate Tool's flow point is great for carving the pieces. The same look can be accomplished with clay tools, compressing the foam instead of melting it.

SUPPLIES

Foam:
  1" sheet, 12" x 12"
  ½" sheet, 12" x 7"
  6" ball
  3½" ball
Paperclay
Foam glue
Acrylic paints:
  Lamp Black
  Dark Chocolate
  Heritage Brick
  Burnt Sienna
BBs

TOOLS

Ruler
Compass
Measuring tape
8 rubber bands
Black marker
Small level
Hot tool with flow point
    & hot knife
Serrated knife
Clay supplies
Sandpaper: 220 grit
Art brushes

Step 8

Step 10

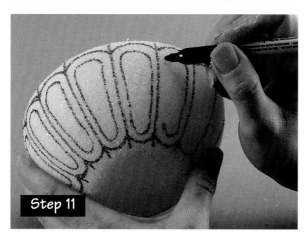

Step 11

Instructions

1. Cut one 7", 6¼", and two 3" discs from 1" foam. Cut one 6¼" disc and one 4" disc from ½" foam.

2. Foam-sand around the outside edge of the discs, making them symmetrical.

3. Foam-sand to round the top and bottom edges. Set discs aside.

4. Mark dot on 6" ball. This will be the top.

5. Measure down 4⅝" from dot all around the ball, forming a dotted line.

6. Cut along line with serrated knife.

7. Cut top ½" off ball, making sure cut is parallel to the bottom. Foam-sand bottom edge to round.

8. Place eight evenly-spaced rubber bands vertically (height) around the dome. Mark along bands, down the side of the dome. Remove bands.

9. Connect lines ¼" up from bottom of the dome with the upward curve.

10. Connect lines ¼" down from top of dome with the downward curve.

11. Draw oval (with a wider bottom) ⅛" inside each set of lines and curves.

12. Hold heat tool just above oval lines, not touching foam, until foam begins to melt. Run tool around each oval to carve grooves.

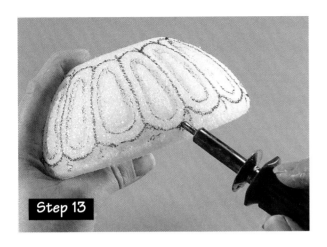

Step 13

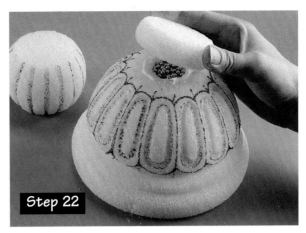

Step 22

13. Run tool along the bottom curve and the area below to "carve" a scalloped edge.

14. Press clay tool ball end or finger press around carved areas to smooth edges.

15. Create hole through center of the dome, 1" wide. This will be filled with BBs later. Set dome aside.

16. Cut off the top and bottom ½" of the 3½" ball. Make sure cuts are parallel.

17. Divide vertically with eight evenly-spaced rubber bands. Mark along bands then remove bands.

18. Press or carve grooves along lines. Smooth edges along grooves.

19. Create a hole through the center of the ball, 1" wide. This will be filled with BBs later. Set the ball aside.

20. Stack pedestal parts in order: 7" disc, 6¼" x ½" disc, dome, 3" disc, 3½" ball, 3" disc, 4" disc

and 6¼" x 1" disc. Check to make sure they are level and all parts fit together well. Sand where necessary. Un-stack and place pieces, in order, in a row.

21. Glue bottom two discs and dome together. Pack dome tightly with BBs.

22. Glue 2¾" disc and 3½" ball in place. Pack ball tightly with BBs.

23. Glue final three discs in place.

24. Check to make sure pedestal is level. Place weight (candle) on pedestal and set aside until the glue is completely dry.

25. Cover pedestal with clay and set aside until completely dry.

26. Sand rough areas and flaws with 220 grit sandpaper. Wipe off dust.

27. Paint pedestal Lamp Black.

28. Dry brush Heritage Brick. Dry brush Burnt Sienna. Dry brush Dark Chocolate.

Sunflower Clock

Skill level: Medium

Cutting and compressing the foam gives this clock its shape, and washes of color add life. This clock was designed to sit on a shelf. For a wall clock, create it using only the front (top) layer. The pattern can easily be enlarged on a copier (up to a 12" width). Hang clock using instructions for wall hangers on page 22.

SUPPLIES

1" foam sheet, 7" x 22"
Paperclay
Foam glue
¾" clock movement
Clock hands
Transfer paper
Paper patterns

Acrylic paint:
Buttermilk
Terra Cotta
Canyon Orange
French Vanilla
Marigold
Cadmium Yellow
Milk Chocolate
2 toothpicks

TOOLS

Pencil
Ball stylus
Serrated knife
Clay supplies
Sandpaper: 220 grit

Instructions

1. Using transfer paper, transfer outside and internal patterns onto foam. No need to transfer inside square on front piece; use it as a guide when attaching front and back pieces. Cut along outside lines.

2. Using a ball stylus, trace around internal lines on front piece: clock circle, turned petal tips and sides of petals. This will make lines easier to see.

3. Use clay tool to compress foam edge next to petal turns. The edges should be sharp, not curved.

4. Compress foam on petals. Work slowly, compressing more each time. Compress where petals overlap, compressing foam deeper where petals meet, and sloping foam to full height at petal tip.

5. Compress foam around clock circle to slope.

6. Compress foam to round petal bottoms and create grooves in petal centers as indicated on the pattern.

7. All edges, except those on petal turns, should be soft and round. Compress to round outside petal edges.

8. Repeat, compressing foam on back piece. The only compressed details are three petal turns and two center grooves.

9. Cut out center square on back piece of sunflower. Foam-sand to round back hole edges.

10. Poke pencil through the clock circle center.

11. Align front and back clock pieces. Push toothpicks through back piece and into front to hold them together.

12. Remove clock parts from movement shaft. Inset the shaft through clock hole. Make sure the battery compartment is on the bottom.

13. The clock should stand on bottom three petals, slightly angling back. If needed, sand the bottom petals until the clock stands correctly.

14. Remove toothpicks and back sunflower piece. Leave clock movement in place.

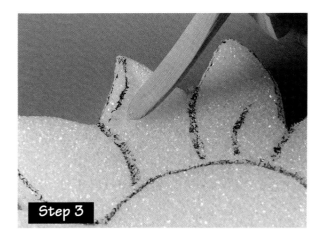

Step 3

Step 4

Step 6

Step 17

15. Trace around movement, then remove it.

16. Enlarge traced square ⅛" on all sides.

17. Compress foam inside square by ³⁄₁₆".

18. Cover top piece with paperclay: front, sides, and tips on backside. To see how much backside to cover, set back piece against it.

19. Cover back piece with paperclay, inside square edges, outer edges and tips on front side.

20. Re-attach front and back clock pieces with toothpicks. Check clock to make sure it stands correctly. Clay can be added to tips of petals if necessary.

21. Remove toothpicks and separate pieces. Cover toothpick holes. Set aside to dry.

22. Sand rough areas and flaws. Wipe off dust.

23. Apply glue to backside of front piece. Press over back piece. Make sure clock stands on bottom three points. Set aside to dry 45 minutes.

24. Base coat center Terra Cotta and petals French Vanilla.

25. On front piece, wash Canyon Orange on leaves, half way up on sides of each petal, and one third up in center.

26. Highlight petal tips and tops of petal turns with Buttermilk.

27. Add shadows in valleys, between petals, and under leaf turns with Marigold.

28. Repeat to add detail to back pieces, ignoring Canyon Orange wash.

29. Brush petals with Cadmium Yellow. This color is very translucent—no need to add water.

30. Wash Buttermilk over tops of petal turns.

31. Dry brush Milk Chocolate in center.

32. Assemble clock mechanism, omitting rubber washer.

Sunflower Clock pattern
Enlarge to 200%

Apple & Pear Clock

Skill level: Advanced

This colorful clock uses both paperclay and joint compound. The compound provides the smooth covering for the foam, and the clay forms the stems and leaves. Only simple skills are needed. Set some time aside to create it, though. Because of the smooth covering, multiple elements, and painting, it does take time.

SUPPLIES

1" foam sheet, 12" x 17"
Paperclay
Joint compound
Foam glue
⅜" clock movement with
    hands
Metal primer
BBs

Acrylic paint:
    Buttermilk
    Terra Cotta
    Country Red
    Hauser Medium Green
    Hauser Light Green
Paper patterns

TOOLS

Black marker
Pencil
Scissors
Small craft knife
Clay tools
Art brushes
Sandpaper: 220 and 400
    grit

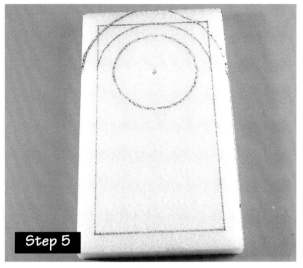

Step 5

Step 12

Step 24

Step 28

Instructions

1. Draw 12" x 7" rectangle on foam. Mark border ¾" in from all sides.

2. Place mark 3½" down from top and 3½" from side. Place compass point on mark for circles.

3. Draw 4" circle.

4. Draw 5½" circle, drawing from side border, across top, to opposite side.

5. Draw 7" circle, drawing from side edge, across top, to opposite side.

6. Cut out plaque along outside lines.

7. With clay tool ball end, trace around inside border line and clock circle.

8. Compress foam inside border, but not clock circle, by ³⁄₁₆".

9. Round edges along border inside and clock circle.

10. Foam-sand to round clock's outside edges.

11. Cut fruit patterns and trace onto foam. Cut out pieces.

12. Foam-sand to slope top edges.

13. Foam-sand ¼" groove in back of the fruit for stem well. Sand to flare top of well out.

14. Place fruit on clock following picture as guide. Make sure fruit fits side by side. Sand apple if needed for better fit.

15. Trace where fruit overlaps border, the pear

on the right and bottom, and the apple on the left. Remove fruit.

16. Compress border foam in overlapped areas ¼", matching depth of rest of compressed foam.

17. Glue fruit in position.

18. Foam-sand bottom of clock, slightly angling it up towards back.

19. Poke pencil through clock circle center.

20. Remove clock parts from movement shaft. Inset shaft through the clock hole. Make sure the battery compartment is on bottom.

21. Trace around the movement, then remove it.

22. Enlarge the traced square ⅛" on all sides.

23. Compress the foam inside square by ¼".

24. Turn the clock to the front and trace around the shaft hole with ball clay tool, slightly indenting and rounding the foam.

25. Draw a rectangle on the back of the clock bottom ½" above bottom, 1" in from the sides of the clock, and 1" tall. Hollow out or compress the foam to be ⅜" deep in rectangle.

26. Fill hollow in back of clock with BBs, making sure to pack them in tightly.

27. Cut 2" x 6" foam piece.

28. Apply glue along outside edge of foam piece and press over hollow, matching bottoms, centering left to right. Let dry 24 hours.

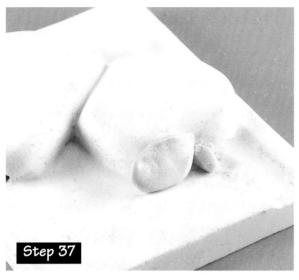

Step 37

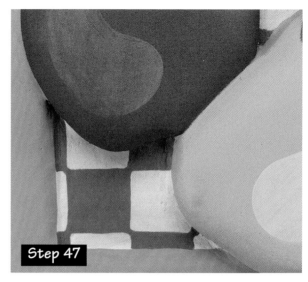

Step 47

29. Foam-sand bottom of clock, making sure it sits flat. Foam-sand to round outer edges of rectangle (covering BBs).

30. Spread on layer of joint compound, brushing back and forth to push compound into foam. Cover front and two side edges. Allow to dry.

31. Apply joint compound to back side and two side edges, let dry.

32. Sand compound smooth with 220 grit sandpaper. Wipe off dust.

33. Brush second layer of compound over front side. Brush back and forth to work mixture into gaps and air bubble holes and to smooth compound. When dry, apply more if needed.

34. Sand compound with 400 grit sandpaper until smooth. Remove dust.

35. To create clay stems, roll ½" ball. Roll into tear shape, bottom ⅜" round and top ¼", 1" long. Flatten top. Dip in water and press in place in stem well.

36. To create clay leaves, roll ⅞" ball. Roll into tear shape; bottom wider, 1¾" long. Flatten to ⅛" thick, smooth edges. Rub water on back and press bottom and tip to pear, using photo as guide.

37. Repeat to create and attach apple leaf. Press leaf bottom to stem, front side to apple and back side to clock.

38. Repeat to add second stem. Set aside until paperclay is dry.

39. Base coat pear in Marigold.

40. Paint highlight Buttermilk. When dry, wash highlight with Marigold.

41. Base coat apple in Country Red.

42. Mix Buttermilk and Terra Cotta for light brown. Paint highlight. When dry, wash highlight with Country Red.

43. Paint clock background Buttermilk.

44. Paint border, sides and back Hauser Light Green.

45. Paint leaves Hauser Medium Green.

46. Pencil in ⅞" squares, centering vertical lines left to right and starting horizontal lines ¼" above bottom border.

47. Paint Terra Cotta squares, rounding corners of Buttermilk squares.

48. Paint ½" Terra Cotta border around clock section.

49. Outline Terra Cotta border with Buttermilk.

50. Paint Buttermilk line with centered square at 12, 3, 6 and 9 o'clock positions.

51. Wash Buttermilk areas with light Terra Cotta wash, using plenty of water. Repeat with second wash. A Buttermilk wash can be used to lighten squares if necessary.

52. Prime clock hands. When dry, paint with Hauser Medium Green.

53. Assemble clock mechanism, omitting rubber washer.

Apple & Pear Clock patterns

Chapter 3

Hanging Around

These projects were meant to hang around adding personality, style, and a touch of fun to bare wall areas. But they don't mind lying down on the job or the support when propped on a shelf.

Letters

Skill level: Easy

Personalize a room with initials, or spell out inspirational words, like "believe," "dream," or "style." Label a room. Spell out your favorite thing. Letters and words evoke a lot of feeling by what they say or by their style. Computers offer many styles, or try the "ransom letter" feel by combining letters of different styles and sizes cut from publications. Enlarge the letters on a copier. Do make sure the letters have a flat bottom if they are to sit on a shelf. And beware of fine detail that will be difficult to cut out of 1" foam.

SUPPLIES
1" sheet foam
Joint compound
Spray paint (Make it Stone® Metallic Gold)
Letter patterns

TOOLS
Scissors
Black marker
Hot knife
Sandpaper: 220 and 400 grit
1" art brush
<u>**Optional**</u>: **Wall hangers**

Instructions

1. Create letter pattern. The letters I used are 10¾" tall. Cut out patterns and trace onto foam. Cut out pieces.

2. Foam-sand to round all top edges. Slightly round bottom edge.

3. Spread on layer of joint compound to front of letters. Brush back and forth to push compound into foam. Allow to dry.

4. Apply joint compound to backside. Let dry.

5. Sand both sides with 220 grit sandpaper until smooth. Wipe off dust.

6. Brush second layer of compound on front side. Brush back and forth to work mixture into gaps and air bubble holes and to smooth compound. When dry, apply more if needed.

7. Sand with 400 grit sandpaper until smooth. Remove dust.

8. Spray paint backs. When dry, spray fronts.

Optional Hanger

See instructions on page 22. Choose angle of letter on wall. Place finger on best location for wall hanger. Turn letter over and press hanger into back, directly across from finger. Make sure to insert hanger prongs toward the top and at a slight angle. More than one hanger can be used, depending on the letter.

Bubbles

Skill level: Easy

Fun and tropical, yet with sophistication that would work in a grown-up bathroom. A foam sheet is cut and compressed to produce the look. Joint compound is brushed and smoothed for the outer shell.

Round bubbles can be created to hang above the fish's mouth. Cut small balls in half, then apply the joint compound using the same steps as the fish. Once sanded smooth, they can be painted and hangers attached to the back following the fish's instructions.

SUPPLIES

1" foam sheet 12" x 14"
Joint compound
Acrylic paint:
   True Blue
   Grape Jelly
   Avocado
   Brandy Wine
   Burnt Sienna
   Raw Sienna
Paper pattern
Wall hanger

TOOLS

Black marker
Scissors
Ruler
Ball clay tool
Hot knife
Sandpaper: 220 and
   400 grit
Art brushes
Paper towels

Instructions

1. Cut pattern and trace on to foam. Cut out fish.

2. Transfer inside pattern lines to foam by lightly tracing with ball clay tool.

3. Use ball end of clay tool to indent line around eye.

4. Indent along outside of curved lines dividing face from body.

5. Compress foam around eye and to left of curved lines, reducing face foam ⅛". Curve side of clay tool works well.

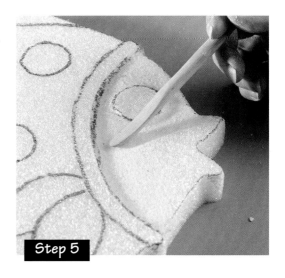

Step 5

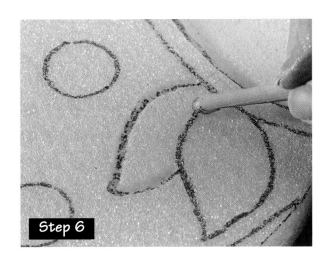

Step 6

Step 9

Step 8

Step 11

6. Trace around body fins to left of face. Create grooves between fins.

7. Note curve before tail. Recess foam ⅛" on entire body, upper and lower fins, stopping at tail curve. Knife side of clay tool works well.

8. Gently angle foam up to tail (which will stay at full height) along curve.

9. Indent ovals on tail, cupping them to ⅛" deep in center.

10. Compress fins by ⅛", above curve on top and below curve on bottom.

11. Indent circles on body, cupping them to be ⅛" deep in center.

12. Foam-sand and finger press to round all edges.

13. Spread on layer of joint compound, brushing back and forth to push compound into foam. Allow to dry.

14. Apply joint compound to backside, let dry.

15. Sand both sides with 220 grit paper until smooth. Wipe off dust.

16. Brush second layer of compound over front side. Brush back and forth to work mixture into gaps and air bubble holes and to smooth compound. When dry, apply more if needed.

17. Sand with 400 grit sandpaper until smooth. Remove dust.

18. Paint body Avocado.

19. Paint face, tail and body circles Grape Jelly.

20. Paint fins, eye and tail ovals Brandy Wine.

21. Paint semicircle between face and body True Blue.

22. Wash Raw Sienna over entire fish. Blot with paper towel to soften.

23. Wash Burnt Sienna over entire fish. Blot with paper towel to soften.

24. Dry brush Raw Sienna wash over Brandy Wine areas.

25. See page 22 for wall hanger instructions. Choose angle of fish on wall. Place finger on best location for wall hanger. Turn fish over and press hanger into back, directly across from finger. Make sure to insert hanger prongs toward the top and at a slight angle.

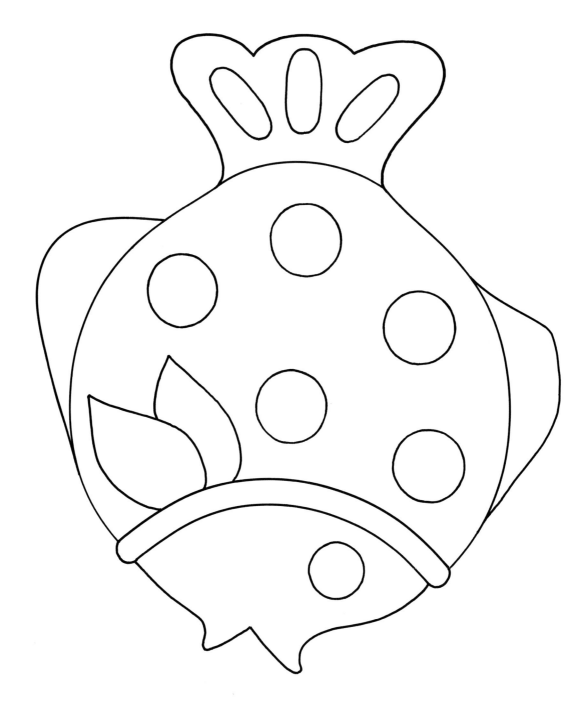

Bubbles pattern
Enlarge to 200%

Fluttery Butterfly

Skill level: Easy

My daughter screamed with delight, "Can I have it?" before this project was even completed. I would have thought this almost-teen was too grown up for butterflies. As I look at it now, I realize that even I still love the wonderful feelings butterflies evoke. I wonder if I dare keep it in my office? Better yet, I'll create two more, changing the color of the stained glass style inserts, maybe even changing the wing slant on each one. She'll be surprised to find a trio of butterflies fluttering in her room one day. And, if I am a good girl, I'll make myself one while I'm at it.

Instructions

1. Cut out wing patterns. Trace two wings from each pattern on to ½" foam, flipping pattern over for second wing. Cut out foam.

2. Rip crepe paper into irregular shaped pieces 1" or smaller. Brush decoupage medium on 1" area of wing. Lay crepe paper on medium. Brush with second coat of medium. Brush on more medium, some over attached crepe paper and some on foam. Lay crepe paper on medium and brush with second coat. Continue to decoupage crepe paper until only edge connecting to body is uncovered. Cover all four wings.

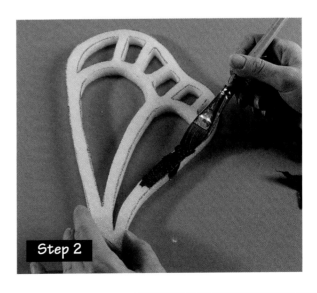

Step 2

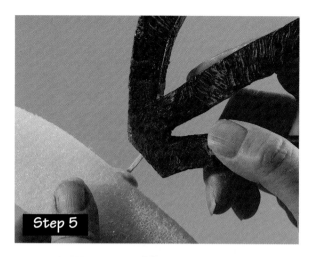

Step 5

Step 12

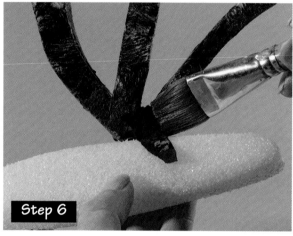
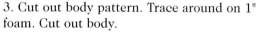

Step 6

Step 13

3. Cut out body pattern. Trace around on 1" foam. Cut out body.

4. Foam-sand to slope edges.

5. Use toothpicks and glue to attach wings to body, wings slightly angling up. Prop up wings until glue has completely dried.

6. Decoupage crepe paper to body. Decoupage pieces overlapping body to wings. Set aside until completely dry, crepe paper will look cloudy.

7. Paint body and wings Lamp Black.

8. Cut along pattern's dotted lines for pattern inserts.

9. For outside edge of wings cut two pieces of yellow tissue from pattern.

10. Cut two red-tissue pieces from each pattern for rest of inserts.

11. Set tissue inserts on wax paper and coat with decoupage medium.

12. When dry, carefully peel from wax paper and turn over on new wax paper. Coat back sides with medium. When dry, peel from wax paper.

13. Spread thin layer of glue onto back of wings, along cut-out edge. Place tissue insert over glue and press in place. Glue all inserts in place.

14. Cut two 6" sections of wire. Follow pattern to bend wire.

15. Insert antennas to top of head, angling outward.

16. Choose angle of butterfly on wall. Place finger on best location for wall hanger. Turn butterfly over and press hanger into back, directly across from finger. Make sure to insert hanger prongs toward top and at a slight angle.

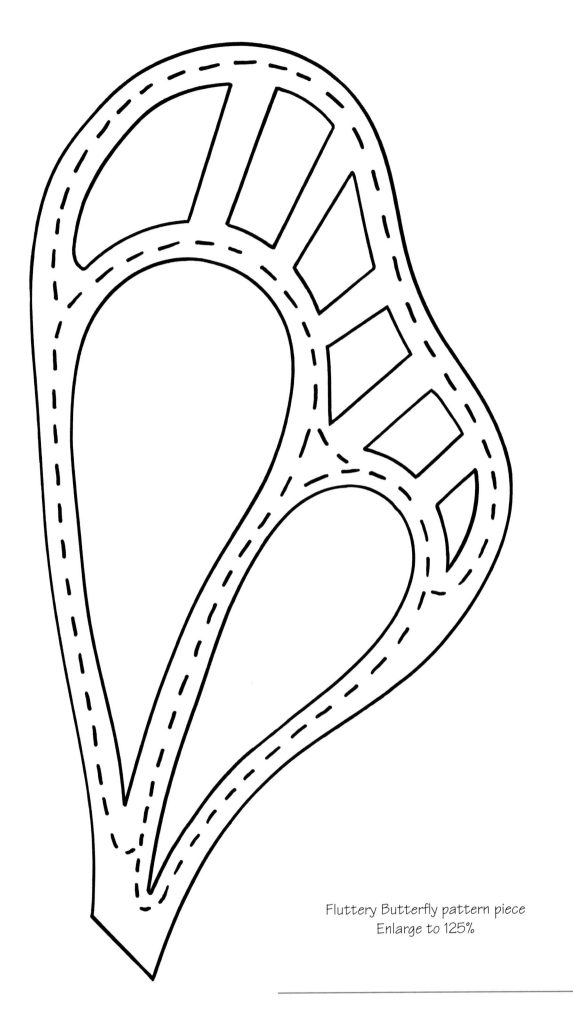

Fluttery Butterfly pattern piece
Enlarge to 125%

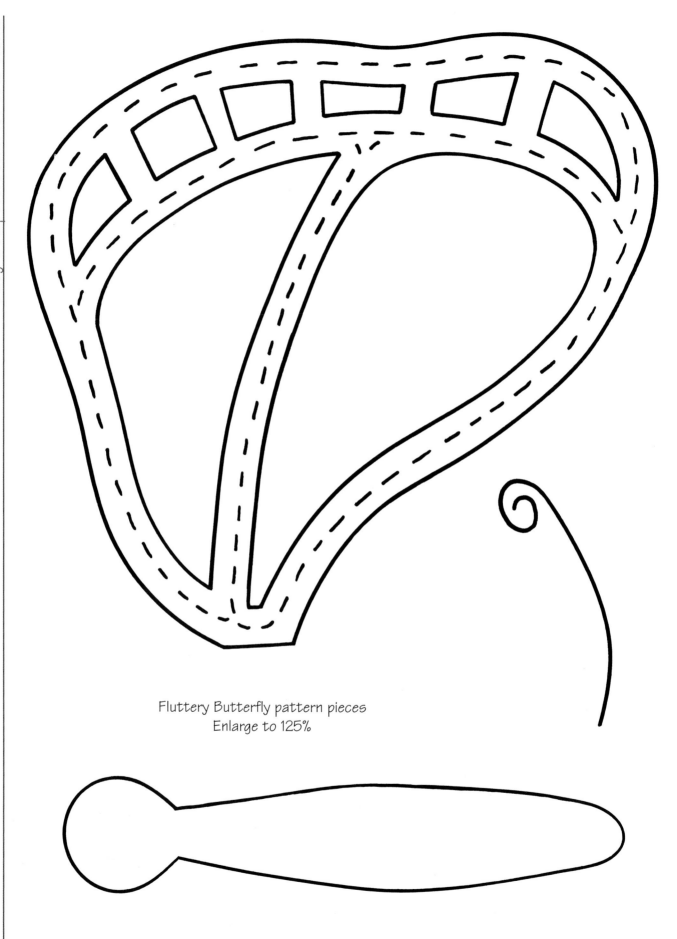

Fluttery Butterfly pattern pieces
Enlarge to 125%

Tree Frog (Stanley)

Skill level: Medium

Stanley's paint treatment was kept simple so it is easy to change. Why change it? So friends can be made. There are actually three frogs in Stan. Slice both patterns in half from head to buttocks. Take one side, make a mirrored copy of it (trace from the backside) and attach the copy half to the original half. Repeat with the second half. Stan has one leg and arm extended. One of his clones will have them all extended, and the other clone will be all tucked in.

SUPPLIES

Foam:
  1" sheet, 12" x 21"
  1½" ball
Joint compound
Foam glue

Acrylic paint:
  Festive Green
  Citron Green
  Leaf Green
  Rookwood
  Lamp Black
Paper patterns
Wall hanger

TOOLS

Black marker
Scissors
Hot knife
Clay tools
1", ½" art brushes
Sandpaper: 220 and 400
  grit

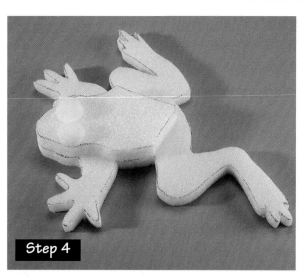
Step 4

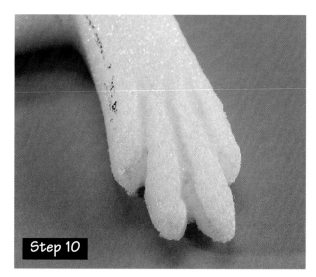
Step 10

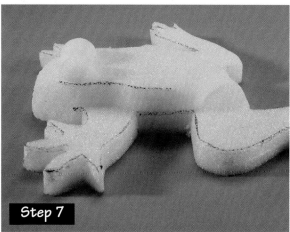
Step 7

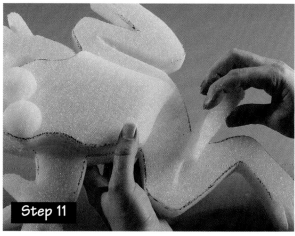
Step 11

Instructions

1. Cut frog pattern and trace onto foam. Cut out.

2. Follow internal solid lines to cut off arms and legs. Trace body pattern on to foam. Cut out.

3. Glue on body piece using pattern as guide.

4. Cut ball in half for eyes. Glue in position using pattern dotted lines as a guide. Let dry 45 minutes.

5. Foam-sand all two layer edges to smooth, making top and bottom flush.

6. Foam-sand to slope back towards buttocks.

7. Foam-sand to slope nose in towards top.

8. Angle fingers and toes to slant down toward tips.

9. Use clay tools to create grooves in toes.

10. Round all finger and toe top edges. Slightly round bottom edges.

11. Foam-sand groove down center of back and on legs using pattern dotted lines as guides.

12. Foam-sand to slope all top edges and round bottom edges.

13. Spread on layer of joint compound, brushing back and forth to push compound into foam. Allow to dry.

14. Apply joint compound to backside. Let dry.

15. Sand both sides with 220 grit sandpaper until smooth. Wipe off dust.

16. Brush second layer of compound over front side. Brush back and forth to work mixture into gaps and air bubble holes and to smooth compound. When dry apply more if needed.

17. Sand frog with 400 grit sandpaper until smooth. Remove dust.

18. Paint frog Festive Green.

19. When dry, apply random color washes of Citron Green and Leaf Green to top side of frog.

20. Paint eyeballs and spots Leaf Green, watered down slightly for transparent coverage.

21. Paint eyes Rookwood. When dry, add Lamp Black pupils.

22. Choose angle of frog on wall. Place finger on best location for wall hanger. Turn frog over and press hanger into back, directly across from finger. Make sure to insert hanger prongs toward the top and at a slight angle.

Tree Frog pattern piece
Enlarge to 200%

Row of Pears

Skill level: Medium

Mother Nature sculpts beautiful and interesting shapes. Trying to mimic her artful touch, five pears were placed in a row for this plaque. The pears and their stems are shaped from foam. The rustic finish, created with joint compound, gives it a bit of European flair. To give it more, break off the edges on the plaque. The look of broken stone adds artistic flair.

SUPPLIES

Foam
  ½" sheet, 7" x 22"
  5⅞" x 3⅞" eggs, 3
1" scraps for sanding
Joint compound
Foam glue
Acrylic paint:
  True Ochre
  French Vanilla
  Buttermilk
  Titanium White
  Sable Brown
  <u>Optional</u>: 2 Wall hangers

TOOLS

Black marker
Ruler
Serrated knife
Sandpaper: 220 grit

Step 3

Step 5

Step 4

Step 6

Instructions

1. Cut foam eggs in half, lengthwise. Only five egg halves will be used, discard one.

2. Cut top ½" off one egg.

3. Place marks around egg, 1½" from top. Connect marks to create line. Repeat to create second line 2½" from top.

4. With 1" thick scrap sand between areas. Angle sanding foam toward 1½" marks to create deeper groove along that line. When complete, groove should be ⅜" at deepest point.

5. Foam-sand above groove to match the depth of the groove.

6. Foam-sand to slope the top of the pear.

7. Foam-sand below groove to create soft curve, from groove to higher center section.

8. Foam-sand on left and right sides to narrow. Sand sides to round.

Step 9

Step 10

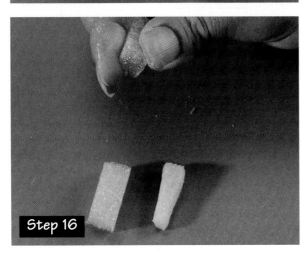

Step 16

9. Foam-sand along bottom to flatten slightly. Sand to round.

10. Sand small groove in top back of pear to mimic hollow for stem. Center should be ¼" across, ¼" deep.

11. Create shallow hollow on pear bottom.

12. When sanding is complete, this pear should be approximately 5¼" tall, 3¾" at its widest point, with the top of the pear 2" across. Repeat to create four more pears, but don't make them exactly the same. Cut off the top of one on a slant, creating groove to match slant. Make one of the necks narrower, wider, or longer.

13. Foam-sand backs of pears.

14. Cut 6½" x 22" rectangle from ½" foam for plaque. Set aside.

15. For stems, cut five ⅜" x 1" pieces of ½" foam.

16. Compress foam by pressing opposite corners in. Form into cone shape, narrowest point ¼", and widest point ⁵⁄₁₆". Set stems aside.

17. Glue pears to plaque, using picture as guide.

18. Glue stems in hollows. One pear stem needs to be glued in its hollow and to the pear it overlaps. Allow to dry 24 hours.

19. Cover pears, front and sides of plaque with layer of joint compound. Allow to dry.

20. Apply compound to back. Allow to dry.

21. Sand pears. Don't over-sand. There will be pits and valleys, yet pears should not feel rough to touch. Foam showing in an area ¼" or larger will need to be re-coated, allowed to dry, and sanded.

22. Basecoat pears and plaque in Antique White.

23. Brush on True Ochre over pears. This is translucent paint, brush on smoothly. Add water to get into nooks and crannies.

24. When dry, dry brush pears with Buttermilk.

25. Highlight areas of pears with French Vanilla dry brush.

26. Wash stems with Sable Brown. Dry brush with Buttermilk.

27. Dry brush Buttermilk over Antique White plaque.

28. Highlight areas of plaque with Titanium White dry brush.

Optional Hangers

See instructions on page 22. Draw line on back of plaque 4" in from left, 1" down from top and ¼" long. Repeat on right side. Press hangers in on each line, hanger prongs toward the top and at slight angle.

Vegetable Plaques

Skill level: Advanced

This project uses foam-shaping techniques to create the main part of the vegetable, and clay skills to create the detail. Sanding is kept very light to add to the rustic nature of the plaques. This series could easily grow: Carrots and eggplant would be a blast—how fun to make cherry tomatoes, squash, and hot peppers!

SUPPLIES

Paperclay
Foam glue
Acrylic paint:
   Lamp Black
   Dark Chocolate
   Burnt Sienna
   Raw Sienna
Paper patterns
<u>*Optional:*</u> *Wall hangers*

TOOLS

Ruler
Black marker
Small craft knife
Serrated knife
Clay supplies
Sandpaper: 220 grit

ONION SUPPLIES

Foam:
   4" ball cut in half
   ½" sheet cut to 6½" x 6½"
   ½" sheet cut to four ¾" x 5¾"

Instructions

1. Mark border ¾" in from sides of 6½" square plaque.

2. Foam-sand along bottom of onion (ball) to flatten slightly.

3. Apply glue to onion's back and press against plaque, centered left to right and bottom ½" above border.

4. Cover onion with thin layer of clay.

5. Smooth clay from onion to plaque.

6. Cover plaque with clay from onion to border. Don't worry if clay gets inside border.

7. Smooth clay along ½" side of frame piece.

8. Apply glue to back of piece. Press against plaque, clay side facing onion.

9. Continue, adding three more frame pieces.

10. Smooth clay along frame's face, above and below onion (sides will be done later).

11. Roll ½" tube 1" long. Press between bottom frame and onion to fill gap.

12. Roll thin tubes for roots. Dip in water.

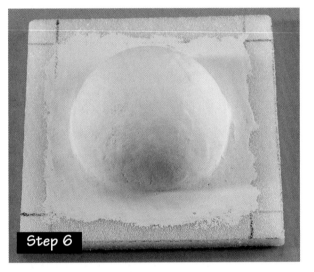

Step 6

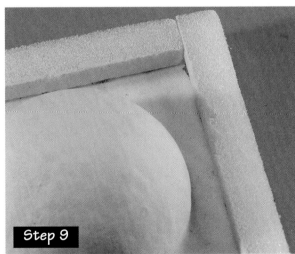

Step 9

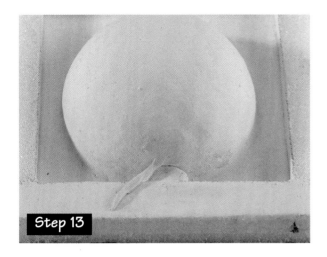

Step 13

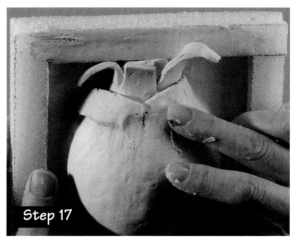

Step 17

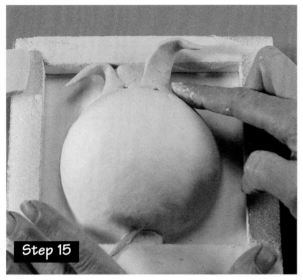

Step 15

Step 20

13. Smooth root tops against bottom of onion. Press them lightly against filler tube and frame. Completely cover sides and front of filler tube with roots.

14. Create rectangle of clay ¾" x ½" x 1". Press between onion top and frame.

15. Cut leaves from ¹⁄₁₆" thick clay. Smooth edges. Dip in water. Smooth leaves to top of onion. Bend leaves using picture for guide.

16. Create ⅝" x 1½" x ¹⁄₁₆" strip. Rip top of strip to be irregular. Place left side against left side of onion, top overlapping bottom of onion's leaves. Smooth bottom of strip to onion. Bend top of strip, using the picture as a guide.

17. Create two strips ⅝" x ¾" x ¹⁄₁₆". Place one to right of strip on onion. Smooth in place. Smooth last strip in place, right edge matching right edge of onion and left edge overlapping second strip.

18. Use end of clay tool to create lines on onion, from top to bottom. Smooth over some areas of lines with fingers to lighten line.

19. Set aside plaque until frame glue has dried.

20. Cover rest of frame with clay. Set aside until clay is dry.

TOMATO SUPPLIES

Foam:
  4" ball cut in half
  ½" sheet cut to 6½" x 6½"
  ½" sheet cut to four ¾" x 5¾"

Instructions

1. Mark border ¾" in from sides of 6½" square plaque.

2. Foam-sand along bottom and top of tomato (ball) to flatten slightly.

3. Foam-sand groove in top back of tomato. Foam-sand edges round.

4. Foam-sand grooves into tomato where indicated in diagram.

5. Apply glue to tomato's back and press against plaque; centered left to right and bottom ½" above bottom border.

6. Cover tomato with thin layer of clay.

7. Smooth clay from tomato to plaque.

8. Cover plaque with clay from tomato to border. Don't worry if clay gets inside border lines.

9. Smooth clay along ½" side of frame piece.

10. Apply glue to back of frame piece. Press against plaque, clay side facing tomato.

11. Continue, adding three more frame pieces.

12. Smooth clay along frame's face, above tomato (sides will be done later).

13. Create six leaves by rolling ⅜" clay balls. Form into tear drops ¾" long. Flatten to ⅟₁₆".

14. Smooth edges. Dip bottoms in water. Smooth leaf bottoms in valley. Bend leaf tips using picture for guide.

15. Roll stem, ¼" wide x 1½" long. Dip one end in water. Push end into valley. Set plaque aside until frame glue has dried.

16. Cover rest of frame with clay. Set aside until clay is dry.

Step 3

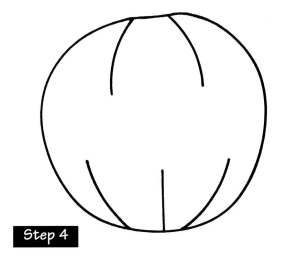

Step 4

Step 4

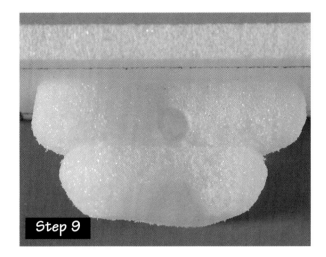

Step 9

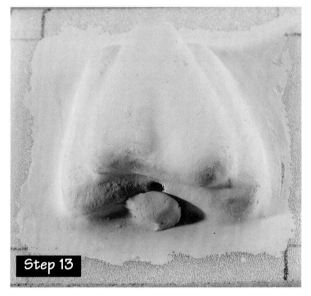

Step 13

Instructions

1. Mark border ¾" in from sides of ½" plaque.

2. Cut top and bottom pepper parts from 1" foam.

3. Foam-sand to slope top edges of bottom piece.

4. Glue bottom piece to plaque, centered.

5. Foam-sand bottom edges of top piece to round slightly.

6. Foam-sand to slope top edges.

7. Sand to create grooves where indicated.

8. Glue top piece over bottom piece.

9. Carve valley into top of pepper for stem, ¼" deep and ½" wide with clay tool.

PEPPER SUPPLIES

Foam:

  ½" sheet cut to 6½" x 6½"

  ½" sheet cut to four ¾" x 5¾"

  1" sheet 4½" x 10"

10. Cover pepper with thin layer of clay.

11. Smooth clay from pepper to plaque.

12. Cover plaque from pepper to border. Don't worry if clay gets inside border.

13. Roll ½" clay ball. Roll into oval. Press against the plaque above the pepper between the two humps on the back piece. Smooth clay against plaque and pepper to form a low hump.

14. Smooth clay along ½" side of frame piece.

15. Apply glue to back of frame piece. Press against plaque, clay side facing pepper.

16. Continue, adding three more frame pieces.

17. Smooth clay along frame's face, above pepper (sides will be done later).

18. Roll ½" tube ¾" long for stem. Dip one end in water. Press in valley. Smooth clay from stem against pepper.

19. Set aside plaque until frame glue has dried.

20. Cover rest of frame with clay. Set aside until clay is dry.

Paint Finish

1. Sand rough areas and flaws. Wipe off dust.

2. Paint Lamp Black, brushing back and forth to push paint into nooks and crannies.

3. Dry brush with Dark Chocolate

4. Dry brush with Burnt Sienna.

5. Dry brush wash of Raw Sienna.

Optional Hangers

Draw line on back of plaque centered left to right, 1" down from top and ¼" long. Press hanger in on line; hanger prongs toward top and at slight angle.

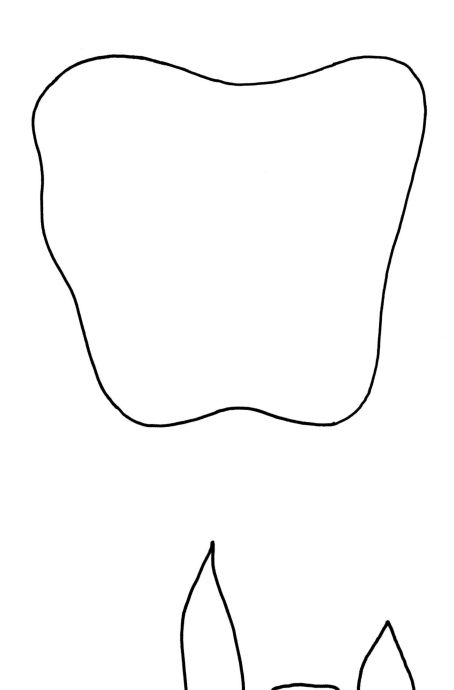

Vegetable Plaques pattern pieces

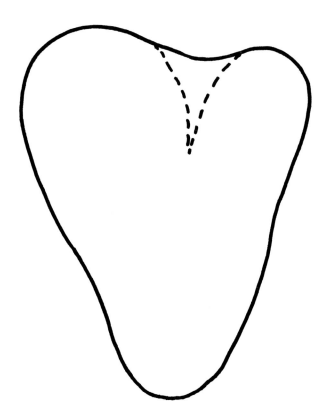

Vegetable Plaques pattern pieces

Chapter 4

Just Because

Just because these projects didn't fit into the theme of any other chapter, they got one of their own.

Roll of the Dice

Skill level: Easy

To create a square box, measurements are important. Remember to keep the blade of the knife straight, not tilted to the left or right. A plastic cup from a liquid medicine bottle makes the perfect template for the circles. If not available, cut a circle from paper and trace.

SUPPLIES

½" foam sheet, 12" x 16¼"
Joint compound
Foam glue
Acrylic paints:
  Brandy Wine
  Fawn

TOOLS

Ruler
Black marker
Compass & scrap paper
Ball clay tool
Serrated knife
Sandpaper: 220 and 400 grit
Art brushes
Plastic tumbler

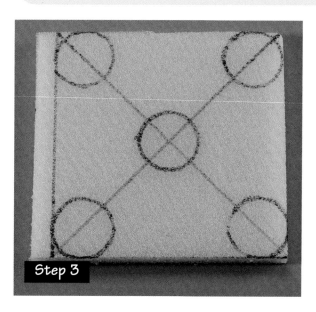

Step 3

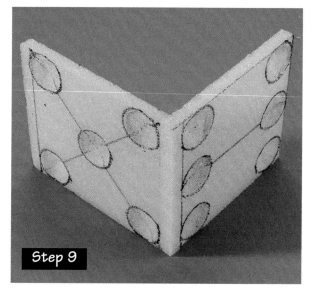

Step 9

Instructions

1. Cut four rectangles 5⅜₆" x 5⅛". These will form sides.

2. Draw line ⅞₆" in from one 5⅛" tall side. This is new side edge; circles will be placed against line.

3. Follow the diagram on page 73 to mark 1⅛" circles on each square, numbers 1, 2, 5 and 6. Circles should be against edges or line. Diagonal lines and center markings can be marked to aid in circle placement.

4. For top and bottom squares, cut two squares 6" x 6".

5. Draw line ⅞₆" in from all sides.

6. Follow diagram on page 73 to mark 1⅛" circles on each square, numbers 3 and 4.

7. With clay tool indent circles, sloping sides down to ³⁄₁₆" depth in center. Curved end of clay tool works well.

8. Each of four side squares will be glued along one side edge and along back of square, next to edge. Apply glue along #5s side edge, opposite line.

9. Press back of line side on #6 against glue, press together.

10. Apply glue along #6s side edge, opposite line. Press back of line side of #2 against glue, press together.

11. Apply glue along the side edge of #2, opposite line.

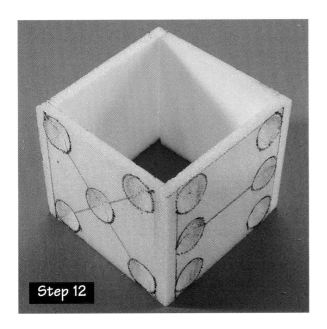

Step 12

Step 16

12. Apply glue along the side edge of #1, opposite line. Press glue edge of #1 against back of line side of #5. Back of line side of #1 will rest on the glue on the edge of #2.

13. Place dice so opening faces up. Check to make sure everything is square.

14. Apply glue around top edges; set #3 on top. Make sure all edges are flush with no side sticking out.

15. Carefully flip dice over. Check again to make sure everything is square.

16. Apply glue around top edges; set #4 on top. Make sure all edges are flush with no side sticking out. Let dry 24 hours.

17. Foam-sand all edges to be flush. Slightly round corners and edges.

18. Place dice on top of plastic tumbler to keep compound on bottom edges from smearing. Cover three sides with compound, brushing back and forth to push compound into foam. Let dry.

19. Cover last three sides, let dry.

20. Sand compound smooth with 220 grit paper. Wipe off dust.

21. Apply second layer of compound, brushing back and forth to work into gaps and air bubble holes and to smooth compound. When dry, apply more if needed.

22. When dry, repeat on next three sides.

23. Sand compound smooth with 400 grit paper. Remove dust.

24. Paint dice Brandy Wine.

25. When dry, paint circles Fawn.

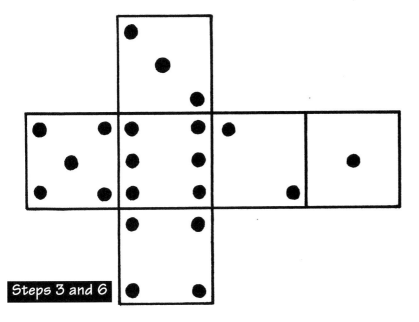

Steps 3 and 6

Pine Tree Grove

Skill level: Easy

Support the trees while working on them to prevent the trunks from snapping. Hold on to them with one hand while brushing on the compound or painting with the other. Working from the top down will help to keep the holding hand clean.

SUPPLIES

1" foam sheet, 12" x 17"
Joint compound
Foam glue
Thick white glue
Acrylic paints:
    Plantation Pine
    Hauser Medium Green
    Light Cinnamon
    Georgia Clay
    Asphaltum
    Fawn
    Honey Brown
BBs
4 toothpicks
4" brown felt circle
Paper patterns

TOOLS

Scissors
Black marker
Compass
Hot knife
Scrap paper
Sandpaper: 220 grit
Art brushes
Plastic tumbler

Instructions

1. Cut out three 4¾" discs.

2. Holding discs together, foam-sand outside edge to make symmetrically round.

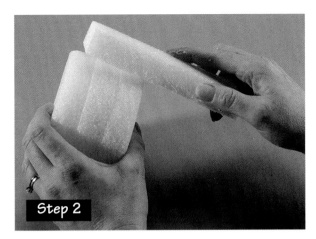

Step 2

Step 9

Step 12

Step 15

3. Foam-sand to round top and bottom edge.

4. Cut out 2" hole in center of one disk.

5. Glue hole disc on top of another disc. Pack hole tightly with BBs.

6. Glue third disc on top. Set aside to dry.

7. Cut tree patterns and trace onto 1" foam. Cut out pieces, trace on to foam and cut out.

8. Foam-sand or finger press edges round.

9. Sand or press branch tips to curve in or down on each side.

10. If desired, bottom of trees can be sanded to tilt left to right or front to back.

11. Put glue on bottom of tree. Stick toothpick half way up trunk. Press other half into base. Repeat with other trees.

12. Stick last toothpick in to tallest tree's trunk; in back, diagonally pointing down, through trunk and into base. Push end of pick in so tip doesn't stick out. Set aside to dry 24 hours.

13. Sand base round, all edges flush.

14. Support trees as you brush on compound. Brush on roughly, with strokes running top to bottom. If compound gets too smooth, allow the compound to set up a bit, then brush again to roughen. Start with tallest tree, working around tree from top to bottom. Make sure compound doesn't build up on edges.

15. Run folded paper in crooks of branches to remove excess compound.

26. Holding on to base, brush 1" band of compound around bottom edge. Brush back and forth to push compound into foam.

27. Set base on tumbler and brush compound on rest of base. Let compound dry thoroughly.

28. Sand base smooth with 220 grit sandpaper. Wipe off dust.

29. Apply second layer of compound on base, brushing back and forth to work into gaps and air bubble holes. When dry apply more if needed.

30. Sand base with 400 grit paper until smooth. Remove dust.

31. Gently rub fingers across textured compound on trees to remove sharp points and loose compound.

32. Paint trees Plantation Pine, let dry.

33. Dry brush trees with Hauser Medium Green.

34. Paint base Light Cinnamon, let dry.

35. Randomly brush light wash (little water) of Georgia Clay over base, working in a crisscross fashion, let dry.

36. Randomly brush light wash of Asphaltum over base, overlapping some Georgia Clay.

37. Randomly wash Honey Brown over base, covering some previous colors.

38. Randomly wash Fawn over base, covering some previous colors.

39. Wash Light Cinnamon over base.

40. Glue felt circle to bottom of base.

Pine Grove pattern pieces
Enlarge to 125%

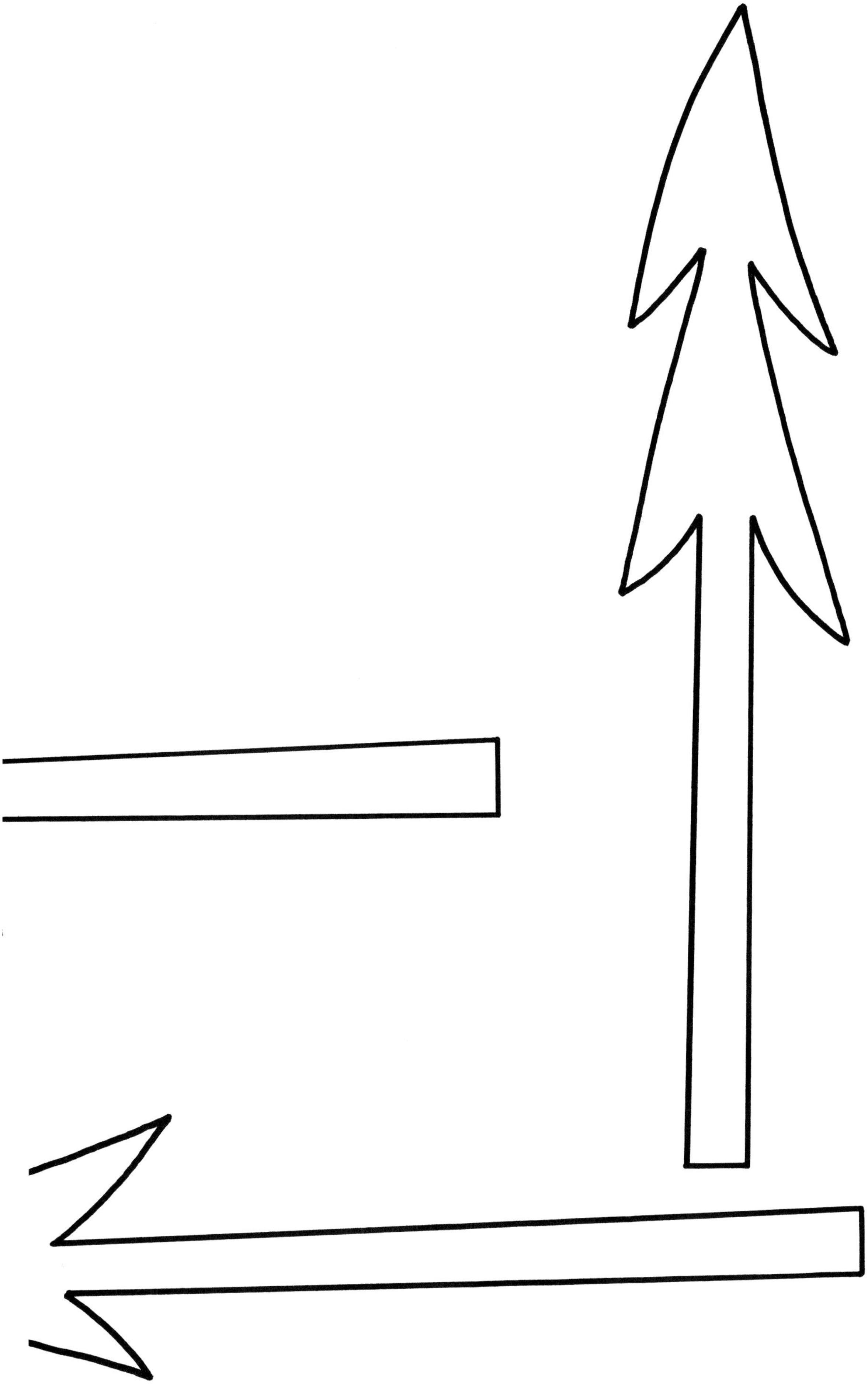

Textured & Imprinted Spheres

Skill level: Easy

This project keeps rolling on … seems as though the more textures you create, more come to mind. Keep the textures from having sharp points that can break off, and be careful not to make the balls lopsided when applying compound. Balls aren't the only option—try cones, hearts, or stars.

SUPPLIES

Foam balls (balls 5" and larger may be difficult to handle)
Joint compound
Acrylic paints:
    Avocado
    Sapphire
    Sand
    Marigold
    Asphaltum

Brandy Wine
Grape Jelly
Dazzling Metallics® in Bronze
Kabob sticks
Leaves

TOOLS

Art brushes
Clay tools
Mist bottle with water
Wire cutters

Instructions

1. Insert stick into each ball.

2. Apply thin coat of compound. Set aside until dry.

3. Apply coat of compound as if spreading frosting.

4. Use brush or clay tools to swirl and pattern compound.

5. For leaf imprint spray ball with fine mist of water. Spray leaf with water.

6. Lay leaf on ball. Press leaf into compound, working from leaf's center to edges. Compound will squish out from under leaf.

7. Remove leaf slowly, from stem lifting up.

8. Repeat to place leaf imprints around ball.

9. Allow balls to dry thoroughly.

10. Gently rub fingers across textured compound to remove sharp points and loose compound.

11. Paint textured balls with Avocado, Sapphire or Brandy Wine. Paint leaf balls with Grape Jelly.

12. When paint is dry, pull out stick or cut off with wire cutters.

13. Fill hole with joint compound (or spackling) and let dry before base coating. Hole can also be left in.

14. For rest of painting, follow steps on one half, let dry before completing second half. Dry brush all balls with Sand.

15. Wash imprinted leaves with Brandy Wine, Avocado, Marigold or Sapphire.

16. Wash all balls with Asphaltum, washing darker in some areas.

17. Dry brush with Sand.

18. Dry brush with Bronze.

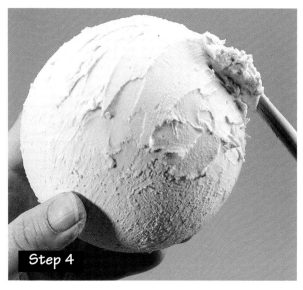

Step 4

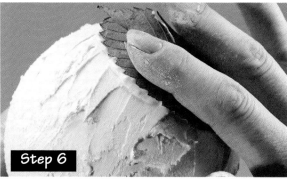

Step 6

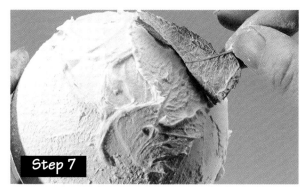

Step 7

Stone Finial

Skill level: Medium

The finial form is created by shaping and stacking pieces. The rustic joint compound texture gives it the look of stone—perfect on a bookcase or mantel.

SUPPLIES

Foam:
   1" sheet for 4¼" disc
   ½" sheet, 12" x 7"
   6" egg
   2" egg
   2½" ball
Joint compound
Foam glue
Acrylic paints:
   Milk Chocolate
   Fawn
   Sand
   Raw Sienna
BBs

TOOLS

Measuring tape
Ruler
Compass
Black marker
Serrated knife
Small craft knife
Sandpaper: 220 grit
Art brushes
Level
Plastic tumbler

Instructions

1. Cut three 2¼" discs from ½" foam.

2. Glue disc in stack. Set aside to dry.

3. Cut one 4¼" disc from 1" foam.

4. Cut two 3" and one 4½" discs from ½" foam.

5. Foam-sand around outside edge of unglued discs, making them symmetrical. Set aside.

6. Measure from egg top down 4" and place mark. Continue placing marks around egg until they form a dotted line.

7. Create a second dotted line 1" down and a third 6½" down.

8. Cut egg along lines. Discard top and bottom pieces. Set aside large top and bottom halves.

9. Foam-sand 4¼" x 1" disc to make symmetrically round. Round bottom edge and slope top edge.

10. Foam-sand both 3" discs to round edges. Set one aside. Apply glue around outside edge. Press centered on 4¼" x 1" disc. This is the start of a base.

11. Cut 2½" ball in half. Discard one half.

12. Cut ball 1" from first cut. Discard small piece.

13. Apply glue around ball's edge, on wider end, press down to base.

14. Cut ¾" wide hole, 1½" deep, in top of ball. Hole will go into disc below.

15. Pack hole tightly with BBs.

16. Foam-sand to round egg top, along cut line.

17. Apply glue to top, turn upside down, and press over BBs. Check finial with level, press on top to make any adjustments.

18. Create 1" wide hole, 1½" deep, and centered in egg. Pack tightly with BBs.

19. Foam-sand to round top and bottom edge of 4½" x ½" disc. Glue over BBs.

20. Carefully turn finial over and check that disc is centered. Carefully turn back over. Check with level.

21. Glue on second egg half, wide end against last disc.

22. Glue last 3" disc on top. Check with level.

23. Hold top and bottom of glued stack of discs, pressing them together. Sand around outside. making edges flush and symmetrically round.

24. With edge of ½" foam, sand middle section until ⅛" deep. If keeping pieces together is difficult, set aside for 24 hours until glue is dry.

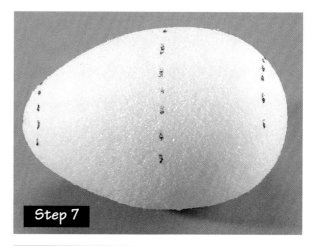

Step 7

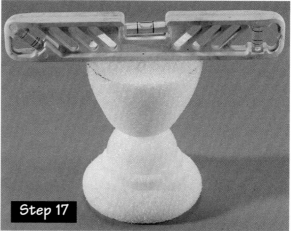

Step 17

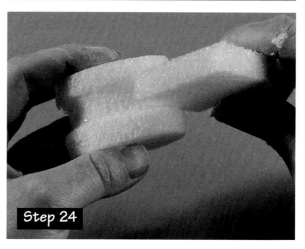

Step 24

25. Tilt sanding foam towards top and sand top part of groove to depth of ¼".

26. Angle sanding disc towards bottom disc and sand lightly to round.

27. Sand around edge of top disc until 1¾" round.

28. Sand bottom edge to soften curve from center to top.

29. Sand to round shape's top and bottom edge.

30. Glue shape on finial. Check with level.

31. Cut bottom ½" off 2" egg.

32. Foam-sand to round cut edge.

33. Glue egg to finial top.

34. Brush coat of joint compound on finial, covering top half. When dry, turn finial upside down in tumbler and finish applying compound.

35. Sand finial. Don't over-sand. There will be pits and valleys, yet finial should feel smooth. Foam showing in an area ¼" or larger will need to be recoated, allowed to dry and sanded.

36. Paint Milk Chocolate.

37. Dry brush with Fawn.

38. Dry brush with Sand to highlight a few areas.

39. Apply Sand wash over entire finial.

40. Apply Raw Sienna wash over entire finial.

41. Dry brush with Sand wash to highlight areas.

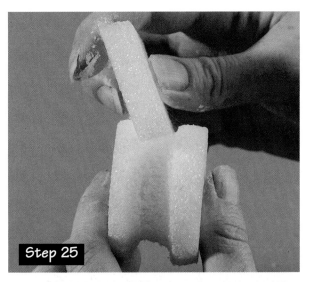

Step 25

Step 28

Step 33

GTR Motorcycle

Skill level: Advanced

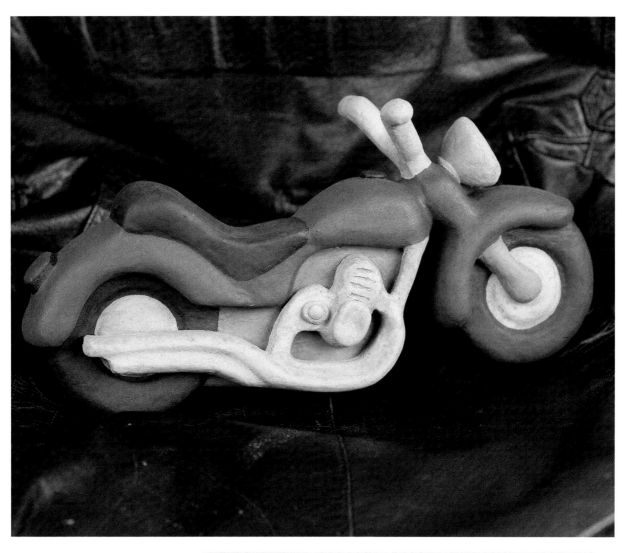

Vroom, vroom. The GTR isn't as difficult as it looks, but it is time consuming. The majority of shaping is done with foam—cutting, sanding and compressing. Paperclay is used to cover the foam and "glue" the various pieces together. Clay tools, damp art brushes, and a ball stylus are a big help in smoothing the clay on this project.

SUPPLIES

Foam:
  ½" sheet, 12" x 12"
  1" sheet, 12" x 5"
  2" egg
Paperclay
Acrylic paints:
  Burgundy
  Neutral Gray
  Slate Gray
  Lamp Black
  Asphaltum
  Country Red

Foam glue
2 toothpicks
Transfer paper
Paper patterns

TOOLS

Ball stylus
Ruler
Hot knife
Clay supplies
Sandpaper: 220 grit
Art brushes

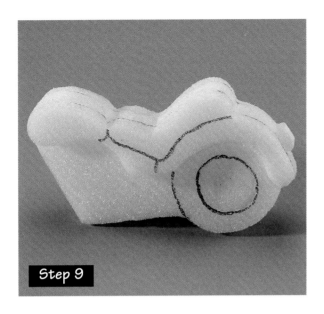

Step 9

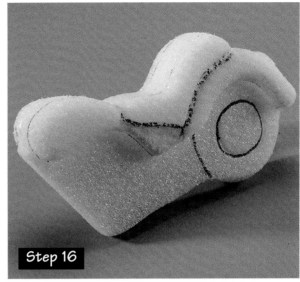

Step 16

Instructions

Shaping Foam:

1. See patterns pieces on pages 90 and 91. Using transfer paper, transfer outside and internal lines of patterns B (Main Body) and C (Front Wheel) to 1" foam. Cut foam out along outside lines.

2. Transfer and cut pattern E (Handlebars) from ½" foam.

3. Transfer and cut two of each pattern from ½" foam: A (Top Detail), F (Bottom Detail), and D (Front Wheel Detail).

4. Glue Top Detail on Main Body, one on each side, matching top edge.

5. Foam-sand to slope top edges on back fender.

6. Foam-sand top edge making joined edges flush.

7. Round bottom edges of fender slightly.

8. Foam-sand bottom end of fender to curve up on left and right side.

9. Foam-sand to slightly round corners and edges of taillight.

10. Press line between seat and fender.

11. Compress foam on fender to match slope on back of fender.

12. Compress area below seat to front of fender, ⅛".

13. Press shallow line between seat and tank.

14. Foam-sand to softly round all edges of seat.

15. Foam-sand top edge making joined edges flush.

16. Foam-sand to sloped edges on tank. There should be a nice curve from side to top and top to bottom and front of tank.

17. Compress foam around the circle in the center of the wheel, indenting ³⁄₁₆" on the line. Slope foam up along the inside of circle, towards center.

18. Foam-sand outside edges of wheel round.

19. Indent foam along outside tire line, separating main body from wheel, compressing foam by ³⁄₁₆" next to wheel and rising to full height ½" from wheel.

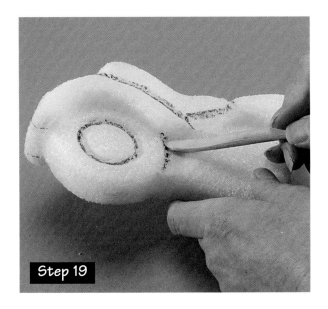

Step 19

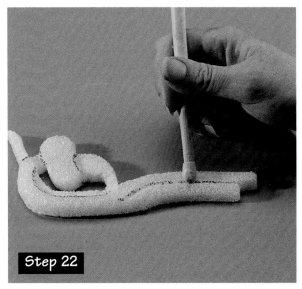

Step 22

20. Foam-sand to slope remaining edges of main body, on bottom and at front of bike.

21. Place each Bottom Detail against bike to make sure which side faces out. Foam-sand to round rest of edges.

22. Groove line between bottom and top exhaust.

23. Compress frame area above exhaust.

24. Compress along exhaust from where it joins engine, and slope to full height where it overlaps frame.

25. Compress frame starting from where it passes under exhaust, and slope to full height ¼" higher along frame.

26. Slightly round the back edges.

27. Set Main Body and Bottom Detail aside to start assembling the front wheel.

28. Compress foam around the circle in the center of the wheel, indenting ³⁄₁₆" on line. Slope foam up along inside of circle, towards center.

29. Compress foam above and below fender by ⅛".

30. Glue Front Wheel Detail pieces to each side of the front wheel.

31. Foam-sand across all pieces, making joined edges flush.

32. Foam-sand outside edges of wheel to round.

33. Foam-sand to slope outside edge on front fender.

34. Round bottom edges of fender slightly.

35. Foam-sand front and back end of fender to curve up on left and right side.

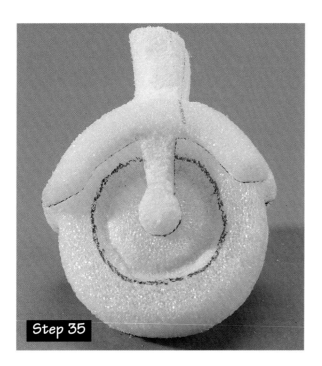

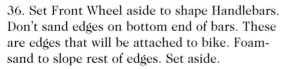

Step 35

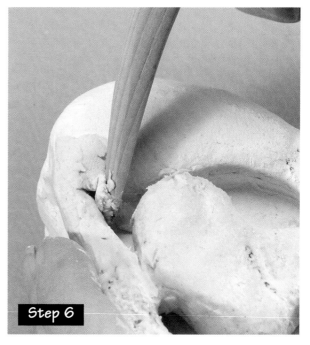

Step 6

36. Set Front Wheel aside to shape Handlebars. Don't sand edges on bottom end of bars. These are edges that will be attached to bike. Foam-sand to slope rest of edges. Set aside.

37. To create headlight, cut 2" egg in half. Discard bottom, rounder side. Press pointed end with finger to flatten slightly. Foam-sand to round cut edge. Set aside.

Note: All foam shaping is complete. Clean-up any dust before starting to cover bike.

Clay Cover

1. Cover Main Body and attached Top Detail with paperclay.

2. Gently cover backsides of Bottom Detail pieces with paperclay. It is best to lay them on a flat surface while doing so. If they break, continue covering. Pieces can be individually attached to bike and covered with clay to hide the break.

3. Flip over and cover tops of pieces. The sides will be covered later.

4. Wet back and press against Main Body, using picture as guide. Bottom and fronts will hang over Main Body.

5. Using clay tools and ball stylus, apply clay to sides of Bottom Detail. Use damp paint brush to smooth clay.

6. Smooth clay from top points of Bottom Detail to tank.

7. Insert ⅛" clay tube, 1" long, between Main Body and Bottom Detail pieces, on bottom of bike.

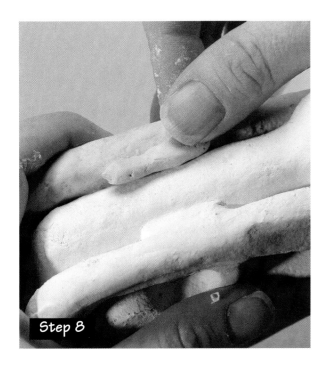

Step 8

Step 12

8. Smooth clay to Bottom Detail and Main Body. Repeat on other side. Bike should stand on its own once Bottom Detail is attached.

9. Press in four lines on upper engine portion.

10. Roll ½" ball of paperclay. Roll into oval. Flatten to ⅛" thick. Press to bottom engine portion.

11. Roll ⅜" ball of paperclay. Flatten to ⅛" thick. Press next to oval.

12. Roll ⅛" ball of paperclay. Roll to oval. Press on top of circle, flattening oval.

13. Cover front wheel with paperclay.

14. To attach Front Wheel to bike, roll tube of clay ⅜" round and 1⅜" long. Flatten to ⅝" x 1⅜". Wet one side and press to Front Wheel in angled area.

15. Rub water on open side. Press against front of bike, squishing clay from rectangle.

16. Insert toothpick through Front Wheel piece, ¼" below top and centered left to right. Push toothpick in until ½" remains out. The headlight will be located here.

17. Make sure bike still stands.

18. Starting at bike bottom and working to top, smooth clay that squished out; smooth some on to the tank and the rest onto the Front Wheel.

19. Cover Handlebars with paperclay.

20. To attach Handlebars, roll tube of paperclay ¼" round and ½" long. Flatten to ⅛" thick. Rub water on one side. Press Handlebar bottom.

21. Rub water on open side. Break toothpick in half. Press one half into bottom of Handlebars, centered front to back and slightly off center left to right.

22. Press Handlebars to top of front wheel, centered left to right and top to bottom.

23. Smooth clay that squished out onto the Handlebars and to the front wheel piece.

24. Cover headlight with paperclay.

25. To attach to bike, roll ³⁄₁₆" clay ball. Flatten to ⅛" thick disc. Smooth edges. Rub water on one

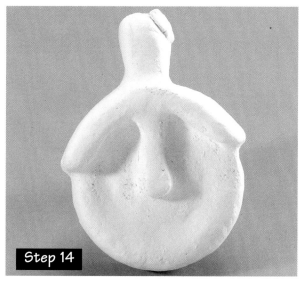

Step 14

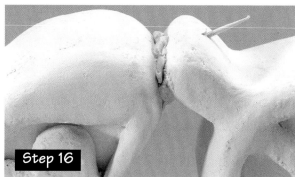

Step 16

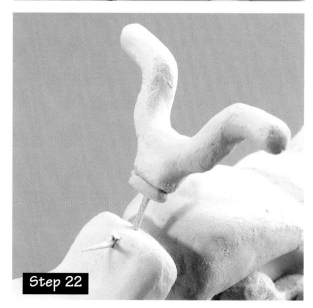

Step 22

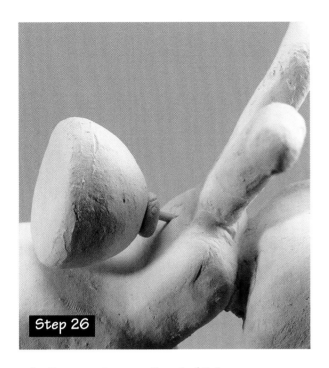

Step 26

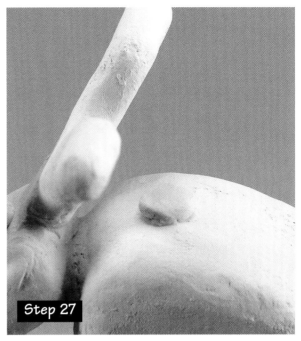

Step 27

side. Press against small end of light.

26. Rub water on open side. Push light over toothpick, against front wheel piece.

27. For gas tank top, roll ⅜" ball. Flatten to ⅛" thick. Press on gas tank, ⅜" from front and centered left to right.

Painting:

1. Using picture as a guide, paint red areas with Burgundy.

2. Paint Lamp Black, Neutral Grey (dark gray) and Slate Gray (light gray) areas.

3. Brush Country Red over Burgundy.

4. Color wash Asphaltum over Country Red.

5. Repeat with lighter wash, more water, over Slate Gray. Brush back and forth to work paint into nooks and crannies.

6. Repeat with heavier wash, more paint, over Lamp Black. Brush back and forth to work paint into nooks and crannies.

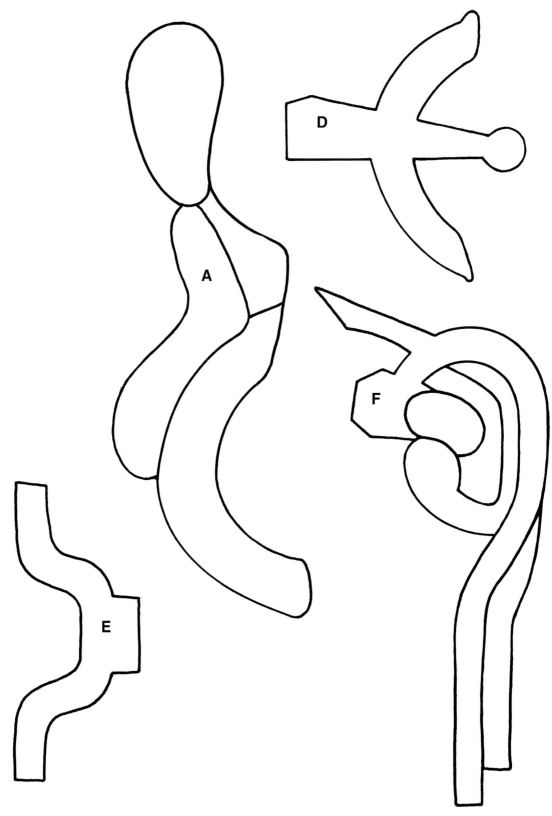

GTR Motorcycle pattern pieces
Enlarge to 125%

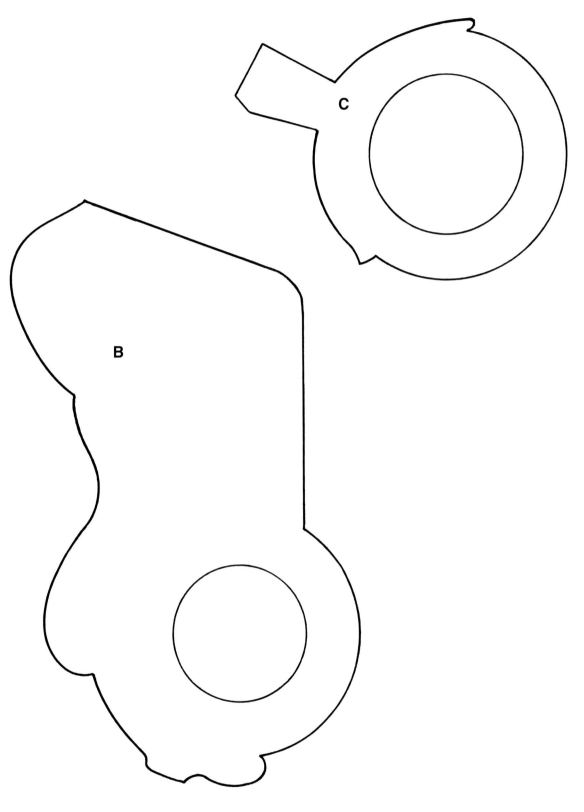

C

B

GTR Motorcycle pattern pieces
Enlarge to 125%

Chapter 5

Sitting Pretty

Art adds color and
life in our worlds.
These characters
brighten the room
by sitting pretty.

Clyde the Alley Cat

Skill level: Easy

SUPPLIES

Foam:
  1" sheet, 12" x 6"
  ½" sheet, 12" x 6"
Joint compound
Foam glue

Acrylic paint:
  Lamp Black
  Buttermilk
  Titanium White
  Neutral Gray
20 gauge black wire, 12"
Paper patterns

TOOLS

Scissors
Black marker
Hot knife
Sandpaper: 220 grit
Art brushes
Wire cutter

This could be a problem project. Not that it is difficult—a hot knife makes it a breeze to cut pieces out. The pieces are then glued together, covered, and painted. This project has one of the shortest supply lists and number of instructions. So what's the problem?

Making these cats is addicting! I made myself stop after three. (There is a picture of all three in the Gallery.) I'd have visions of a Siamese one. And wouldn't a soft gray one look good with the crew? I've always wanted a tortoise shell cat. I might be in danger of becoming a "cat lady."

To change the head angle, cut the pattern along dotted line. Tilt and tape back to body.

Instructions

1. Cut cat patterns (page 94), and trace them onto foam sheets: main body on 1" and tail on ½". Cut out pieces.

2. Follow interior lines to cut out the nose and legs. Trace onto ½" foam sheet. Cut out.

3. Using the picture as a guide, glue nose, front legs, and tail on to body. Let dry 45 minutes.

4. Foam-sand edges to round slightly.

5. Brush joint compound on front and sides. Brush back and forth and in a swirling motion to push compound into holes. Make sure to cover foam well. Don't over-brush or the compound will become smooth. To correct this, allow compound to set. Brush again to roughen. Let dry.

6. Brush compound onto backside. Make sure not to create ridges with compound on edges. Let compound dry thoroughly.

7. Gently rub fingers across textured compound to remove sharp points and loose compound.

8. Sand nose and bottom smooth, making sure cat sits flat.

9. Follow picture to paint light areas Buttermilk.

10. Paint rest of cat Lamp Black.

11. Dry brush Titanium White over Buttermilk.

12. Dry brush Neutral Gray over Lamp Black.

13. Cut six wire whiskers 2" long.

14. Insert one on right of nose, ⅛" from back and ⅛" from bottom of nose.

15. The second whisker is placed ⅛" from front and ⅛" from bottom.

16. The third whisker forms the point of triangle, ⅛" above and centered over others.

17. Repeat on right side.

Clyde the Alley Cat pattern pieces
Enlarge to 125%

Colonel Sanders

Skill level: Easy

Colonel Sanders is the classic, all-American rooster. The foam is shaped by cutting, sanding, and compressing grooves. The paperclay covering is painted to look weathered.

SUPPLIES

Foam:
  6" ball
  1" sheet 12" x 6"
Paperclay
Foam glue
4 toothpicks
Paper patterns

Acrylic paint:
  Light Avocado
  Uniform Blue
  Georgia Clay
  Deep Burgundy
  Antique Gold
  Light Buttermilk
  Fawn

TOOLS

Measuring tape
Black marker
Scissors
Large rubber band
Serrated knife
Small craft knife
Clay supplies
Sand paper: 220 grit
Art brushes

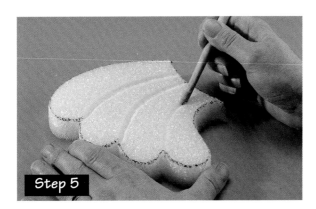

Step 5

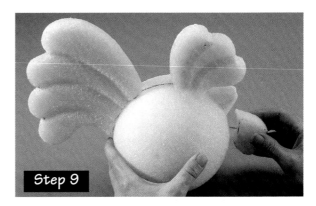

Step 9

Instructions

1. Cut bottom ½" off ball.

2. Place rubber band around ball dividing it in half vertically (left to right). Mark line and remove rubber band.

3. Cut waddles, tail, and beak pattern, and trace onto 1" foam sheet. Cut out pieces.

4. Place pattern on pieces and transfer inside lines with ball clay tool. Flip pattern pieces and foam over to transfer lines to second side.

5. Use clay tools to press grooves along lines.

6. Finger press to smooth grooved edges.

7. Leaving edges of attachment side square, foam-sand rest of edges to round.

8. Apply glue along attachment side of bottom waddle. Insert toothpick half way into attachment side, centered. Press toothpick into foam ball, on marked line. Press firmly. Note: Use picture for placement guide. The rooster will tip if its tail isn't far enough forward.

9. Repeat to add beak (use ½ of toothpick instead of full one), second waddle, and tail.

10. Transfer wing pattern, one to each side. Use clay tools to press groove along lines. Allow glue to dry 24 hours.

11. Cover form with clay. Allow to dry.

12. Sand rough areas and flaws. Wipe off dust.

13. Paint body Fawn, tail Light Avocado, wings Uniform Blue, beak Georgia Clay, and waddles Deep Burgundy.

14. Mix wash of Antique Gold. Paint stars on wings, beak, and waddles.

15. Wash Fawn over tail, wings, beak and waddles.

16. Wash Light Buttermilk over body.

17. Wash over all body parts with original color.

18. Wash Antique Gold over body.

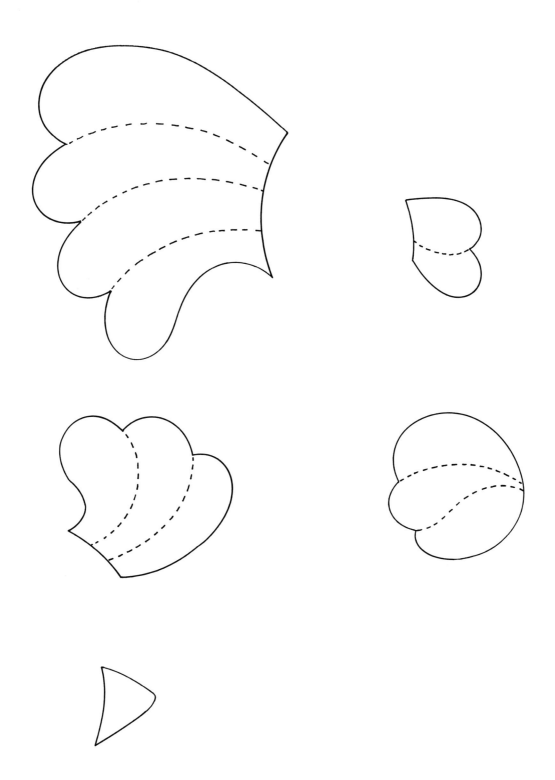

Colonel Sanders pattern pieces
Enlarge to 200%

Gus

Skill level: Medium

Owls were everywhere when I was growing up. If you wanted to give my mom the perfect present, you found her a uniquely sculpted owl (along with a box of chocolate-covered cherries). Gus, the first in my collection, brings thoughts of my mom to me.

He was handled a bit too much when he was wet causing him to stand a bit off-kilter. And one of his ears isn't quite like the other ... I guess he has a bit of me in him, too.

SUPPLIES

3½" foam ball
Paperclay
Acrylic paints:
  Lamp Black
  Buttermilk
  Raw Sienna
  Metallic Bronze

TOOLS

Scissors
Ruler
Serrated knife
Clay supplies
Sand paper: 220 grit
Art brushes

Step 1

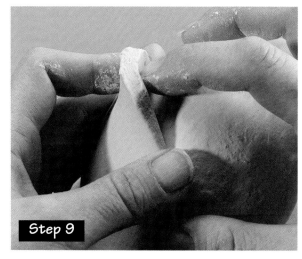

Step 9

Step 3

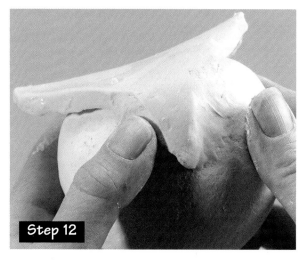

Step 12

Instructions

1. Cut a ½" deep wedge from top of ball.

2. Foam-sand to round cut edges.

3. Foam-sand center front of head; rounding from top of head to widest part of ball.

4. Cover foam with clay.

5. Cut pattern from ¼" thick clay. Smooth clay edges.

6. Place pattern on head; pattern back against top back of head and beak tip 1½" from bottom of ball.

7. Smooth clay from pattern to back of ball for 2" along center.

8. Lightly press along center pattern to make sure it's resting against ball.

9. Place finger under an ear, pull up slightly and press in on each side of ear. This will curve inside of ear.

10. Repeat with second ear.

11. Pull up on center of each ear causing tips to slope up.

12. Smooth clay along beak, for 2" on each side.

13. Roll clay tube ¼" x 3½" to outline eye area. Rub water along back. Set tube to right of nose, just above beak tip.

14. Curve tube into arch; down and to left, up along side of face, into bottom of ears (2" above beak tip). Trim tube if necessary.

15. Press tube against face, flattening slightly.

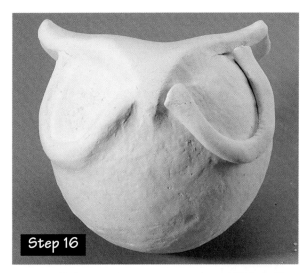

Step 16

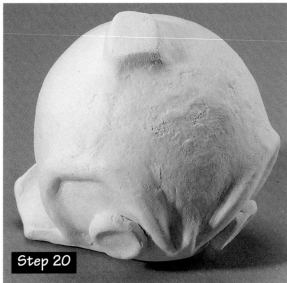

Step 20

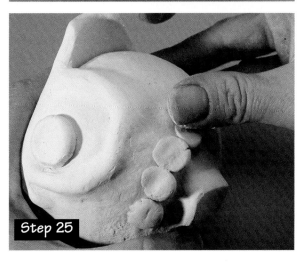

Step 25

16. Smooth tube to head along inside and out-side edges.

17. Create ½" ball of paperclay. Flatten to ¼" disc. Dip back in water.

18. Position disc in eye area. Press in center to attach and indent center.

19. For leg, roll ½" x 1" tube. Dip 1" side in water.

20. Place against bottom of owl, centered top to bottom and ⅛" to left center. Smooth all sides to body.

21. Repeat for second leg, placing to right of center.

22. Set owl on flat surface. Press down on head until owl sets flat.

23. For feathers, create ¼" clay balls. Flatten slightly into discs. Dip back in water.

24. Place first disc ½" above feet, centered. Flatten disc top against owl.

25. Continue creating and placing feathers. Work around bottom of owl in circle. Offset feathers on second row. Use smaller feathers in front, along eyes and beak. Use larger ones on back.

26. If necessary add clay to beak to build it up higher than feathers. Let clay dry.

27. Sand rough areas and flaws on flat parts of owl.

28. Paint Lamp Black.

29. Dry brush Light Buttermilk.

30. Dry brush Raw Sienna.

31. Dry brush Light Buttermilk on feather tips and ear tips.

32. Dry brush Bronze. Bronze is transparent, so keep brush slightly wet with paint.

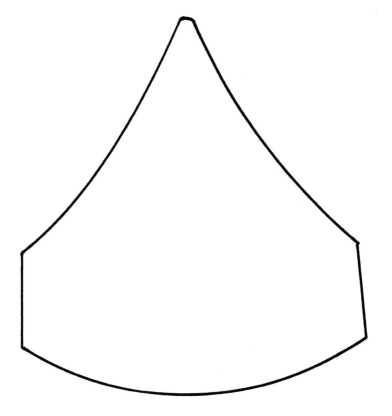

Gus pattern piece

Cow Herd

Skill level: Advanced

The herd is on its way home! One of the group is checking the sky, wondering if they'll make it home before the old farmer wakes up. Or maybe she's taking a look at the moon and deciding if she wants to make one last jump.

SUPPLIES

Foam:
  4" and 2" foam balls
  2½" egg
  1" sheet, 12" x ⅞"
Paperclay
Acrylic paints:
  Bittersweet Chocolate
  Khaki Tan
  Light Buttermilk
5 toothpicks
Paper patterns

TOOLS

Black marker
Scissors
Ruler
Serrated knife
Small craft knife
Clay supplies
Sand paper: 220 grit
Art brushes

Step 2

Step 6

Step 3

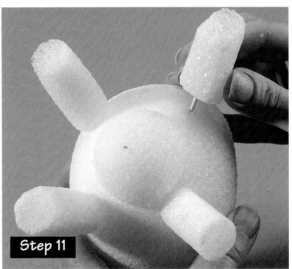

Step 11

Instructions

1. For body, cut ⅝" off top of ball.

2. Set body on work area, cut end facing forward. Slice off each side, angling knife tip in and handle away from body. Back should be about 2" wide and belly full-size.

3. Slice or foam-sand center of back so it slightly curves down.

4. Foam-sand ball to slope cut edges.

5. For milk sack, cut 2" ball in half. Set one side aside for use on another cow.

6. Curve flat part by pressing down and rubbing with clay tool. Curve flat part in until it rests against the cow's belly.

7. Glue in place, centered.

8. Cut four blocks from 1" foam; ⅞" x ⅞" x 2".

9. Cut out leg pattern. Place on top of blocks and cut top and bottom off.

10. Foam-sand edges, forming tubes. Finger press to lightly round bottom edge.

11. Insert toothpick into tube top, then push into belly. Position leg ¼" away from milk sack; top leg point angling away from center of milk sack.

12. Glue all legs to body.

13. For head, cut ¼" off narrow end of egg. This will be the nose end.

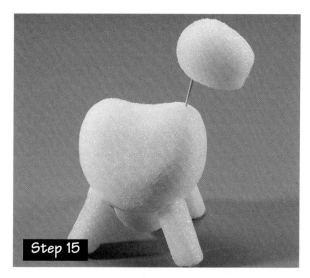

Step 15

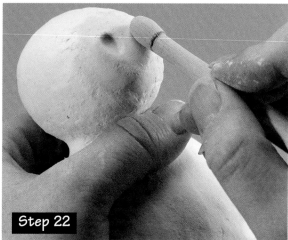

Step 22

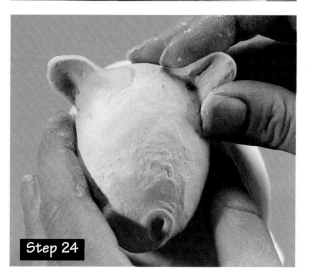

Step 24

14. Insert toothpick half way into head; 1" down from wide end of egg.

15. Apply glue around toothpick; insert toothpick into body.

17. Apply clay to legs, then belly.

18. Create teats with ¼" balls of clay smoothed to udder.

19. Continue smoothing clay to body. Smooth clay to head.

20. Create nose by rolling ¾" clay ball. Flatten until 1" wide. Push to head and smooth clay from sides to head.

21. Push nose into egg until sides flair out slightly.

22. Push top of nose against egg more. Create nostrils with clay tool.

23. Cut two ears from ³⁄₁₆" thick clay. Push ear bottoms to head. Smooth clay from ear bottom to head.

24. Use clay tool to curve inside of ears. Pinch ears in on each side just above head.

25. For horns, roll ⅛" x 2¼" clay tube. Roll ends into soft points. Press center of tube to head, centered between ears. Smooth bit of clay to front of head, smoothing majority to back of head.

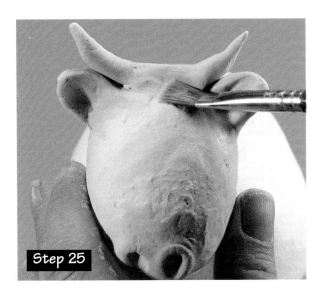

Step 25

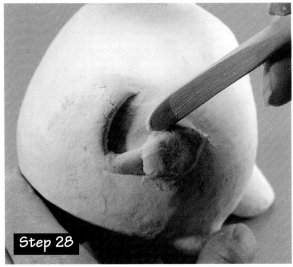

Step 28

26. Curve horns up.

27. For tail, roll ⅛" x 2" tube. Smooth one end of tube to the cow's back. Let tail fall down buttocks and then curl to side.

28. Cut tail's end from ³⁄₁₆" thick clay. Smooth end to tail and sides to body. Allow clay to dry.

29. Sand rough areas and flaws. Wipe off dust.

30. Paint cow Khaki Tan.

31. Dry brush wash of Light Buttermilk.

32. Paint triangles, squares, or circles with two coats of Bittersweet Chocolate.

33. Dry brush Khaki Tan over shapes.

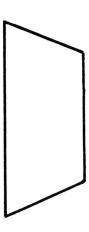

Cow Herd pattern pieces

A Dinosaur Named Drake

Skill level: Advanced

Wouldn't it be nice if dinosaurs weren't pictured as drab, ugly creatures? Drake prefers a more colorful world. And he has such a great personality that even if the shaping or clay forming isn't perfect, he still looks good.

SUPPLIES

Foam:
6", 4", 2½" and
2" egg
1" sheet 6" x 12"
Foam glue
Paperclay
5 toothpicks
Paper patterns

Acrylic paints:
Wedgewood Blue
Desert Turquoise
Grape Juice
Moon Yellow
Citron Green
Bright Orange
Royal Fuchsia

TOOLS

Ruler
Scissors
Black marker
Hot knife
Serrated knife
Sand paper: 220 grit
Clay supplies
Art brushes

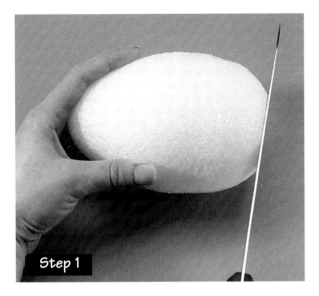

Step 1

Step 5

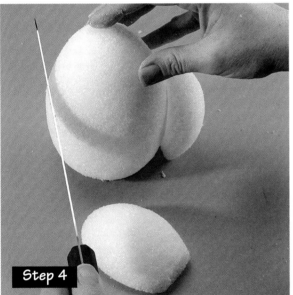

Step 4

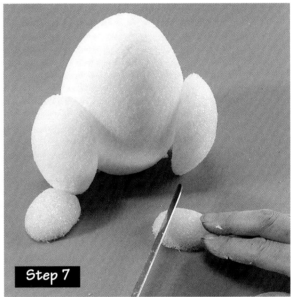

Step 7

Instructions

1. Slice bottom off 6" egg, angling cut from ½" in back to slightly less in front. The egg (Drake's body) will sit slanting forward.

2. For legs, cut top ¼" off of the 4" egg. Cut egg in half vertically. Sand with foam to round side cut edges. Egg's bottom (widest part) is the top of leg.

3. Set body egg on flat bottom. Each side will need flat area to attach leg. Set leg against egg to see where to cut.

4. Cut thin slice off each side, angling knife tip away from egg, cutting more off in front. Check fit of leg. If needed, sand or slice off more foam.

5. Use toothpicks and glue to secure legs.

6. For feet, cut 2" egg in half vertically (top to bottom).

7. Set each foot in front of leg, wide part of egg against leg and angling feet outward. Note angle on bottom of leg. Cut back of feet at matching angle; cutting more off foot top and slanting to less at foot bottom.

8. Use toothpicks and glue to secure feet to legs.

9. Cut out spike pattern on page 110 and trace on 1" foam. Cut spikes.

10. Finger press or sand to round spike edges. Don't sand edges to be attached to body.

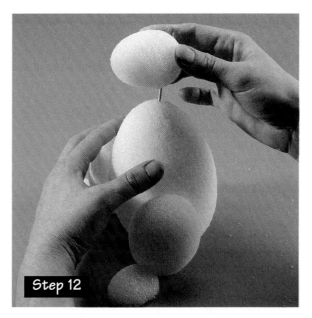

Step 12

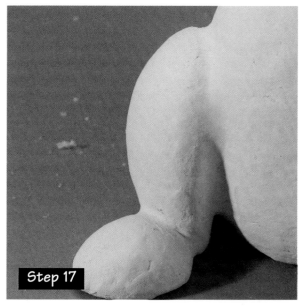

Step 17

Step 15

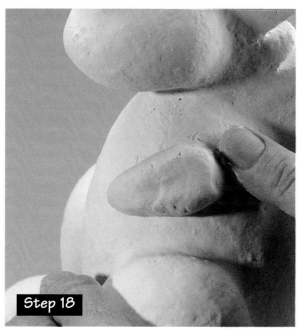

Step 18

11. Round spike tips, lower on left and right side.

12. Insert toothpick half way into 2½" egg head, 1" down from widest end.

13. Apply glue around toothpick; insert toothpick into body, tilting nose end slightly down.

14. Check fit of spikes. If necessary, sand along spikes joining edges. Small gaps can be filled in with paperclay.

15. Glue spikes, centered, down back of head and body. Allow glue to dry 24 hours.

16. Cover foam with paperclay. Fill gaps where needed; between body and spikes and foot and leg.

17. Add clay to create smooth transition between leg and body.

18. Roll 1" clay ball for arm. Form into tear drop shape 2" long. Press wide end against body. Smooth clay to body along shoulder area.

19. For fingers, roll thin tubes of clay ⅜" to ¾" long. Taper ends. Attach to arm.

20. Repeat for second arm. Allow clay to dry.

21. Sand rough areas and flaws. Wipe off dust.

22. Paint Drake Wedgewood Blue.

23. Wash with Desert Turquoise.

24. Dry brush with Grape Juice, Moon Yellow, Citron Green, Bright Orange and ending with Royal Fuchsia.

25. Paint large Citron Green spots on body. Put small dots on finger tips. Citron Green is a translucent color. Put on strokes as smoothly as possible.

26. Paint small spots on body with the rest of colors.

27. Paint spike border with Citron Green.

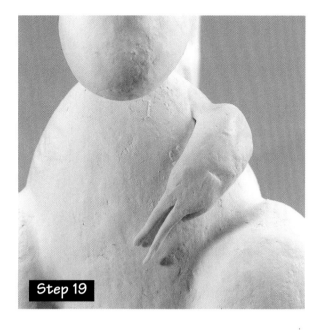

Step 19

Dinosaur pattern piece

Gracie

Skill level: Advanced

SUPPLIES

Foam:
   6" egg
   2½" ball
   1" sheet 12" x 1¼"
Paperclay
Foam glue
Acrylic paints:
   Wedgewood blue
   Canyon Orange
   Light Buttermilk
   Golden Straw
   Deep Burgundy
   Raw Sienna
Decorator paste
14 gauge galvanized steel
   wire, 23"
Three feathers
Small button with loop
Paper patterns

TOOLS

Wire cutter
Needle nose pliers
Thick white glue
Scissors
Serrated knife
Small craft knife
Clay supplies
Sand paper: 220 grit
Art brushes

It was a classic story. Gracie always dreamed of leaving the barnyard. There was more for her somewhere else. She would listen intently as the crazy Goose told stories of "The City." The others would laugh, but Gracie knew she belonged there. She could picture herself in every story with the hustle, bustle, and beautiful sights. She felt it in every part of her being. She struggled to save everything she could, knowing one day she would have enough for a new hat. Then off she would run.

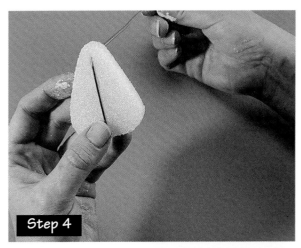

Step 4

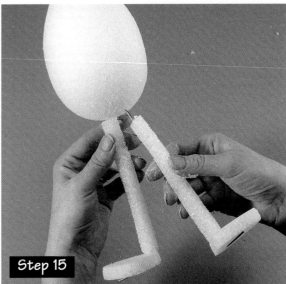

Step 15

Step 22

Instructions

1. Cut two pieces of 8½" wire.

2. Bend each piece of wire 1¾" from end at 90 degree angle, forming "L."

3. Cut out feet pattern and trace on 1" foam. Cut out feet.

4. Push long straight wire end through foot bottom ¼" in from heel, centered.

5. Pull wire through foot until bent section rests centered on foot bottom. Press bent section into foam.

6. Repeat with second foot and wire.

7. Cut 1" foam piece, ⅝" wide and 5¼" long. Slice off ¼" of 1" thickness resulting in ⅝" x ⅝" rectangle.

8. Foam-sand edges creating ½" tube.

9. Push leg wire through center of foam tube.

10. Pull tube up, away from foot. Apply glue to bottom of tube. Push tube back against foot.

11. Repeat for second leg.

12. Push wire above leg into egg bottom; slightly to one side of center point, bottom of leg angling out.

13. Repeat with second wire, going slightly to other side of center.

14. Holding on to legs, push egg slightly back until form stands on its own.

15. Pull legs wires out. Apply glue to top of leg foam. Push wires firmly back in place. Note: Connection between legs and eggs must be strong or there will be difficulties when applying clay.

16. Cut 6" wire for neck. Bend to match pattern.

17. Press straight wire end into egg top, centered. Press other end into ball.

18. Cut 1" foam into rectangle, ¾" square and 4" long.

19. Foam-sand edges creating ⅝" tube.

20. Cut one ½" piece from tube. Slice halfway through this disc, apply glue to bottom.

21. Place slit against neck wire. Push until wire is in center of foam. Push disc down against body.

22. Continue adding ½" pieces (cut some into wedges to accommodate for curves) until neck wire is filled. There will be extra foam left from tube.

Step 27

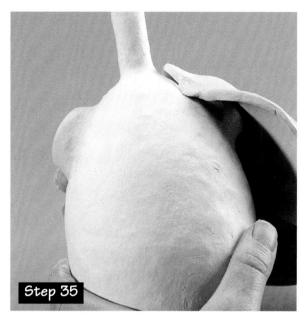

Step 35

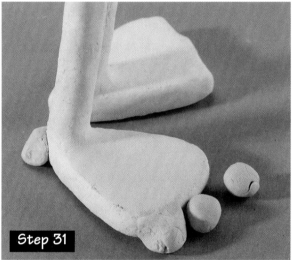

Step 31

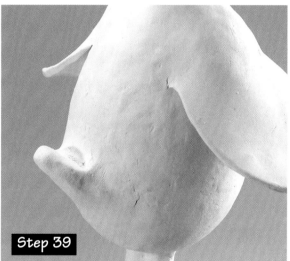

Step 39

23. Neck and leg foam provides much support for the bird. Allow glue to dry for 24 hours before applying clay.

24. Apply clay to body, head, and then neck.

25. Cut out beak from ⅛" thick clay. Smooth edges.

26. Fold beak in half. Press against head and smooth beak corners to head.

27. Roll two tubes of clay ⅛" thick and 1¼" long. Place one above and one below beak. Smooth half of each tube to beak and other half to head.

28. Cover legs and feet with clay.

29. Roll three ½" clay balls.

30. Press balls to front of feet to form toes. Smooth in place.

31. Roll ½" clay ball. Smooth to back of foot for a heel.

32. Cut out two wings from 3⁄16" thick clay. Smooth edges.

33. To create support for the wing, roll 1" ball. Flatten to ⅜" disc.

34. Rub water on back of disc. Press to shoulder area, further flattening to ¼" thick. Smooth clay to body.

35. Set wing over support and smooth top part of wing to body.

36. Repeat to create second wing.

37. Cut tail from ½" thick clay. Smooth edges.

38. Press tail in place. Use picture for guide.

39. Press on tail buckling clay against body. Smooth clay from buckle to body.

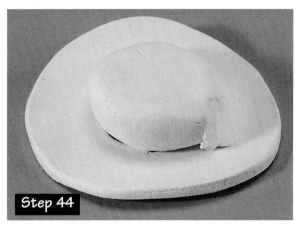

Step 44

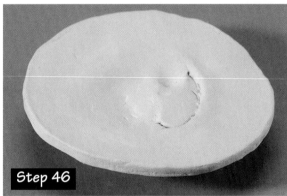

Step 46

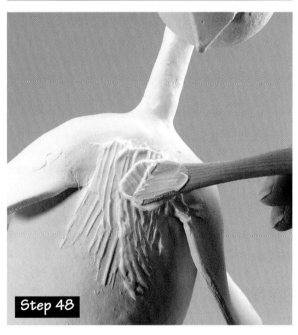

Step 48

40. Make sure form stands on own. Clay can be added to feet bottoms if necessary. Set aside to dry.

41. Cut out hat rim from ⅛" thick clay.

42. Roll clay into 1½" clay ball. Flatten to ½" thick disc.

43. Place disc centered over hat rim.

44. Smooth clay from disc sides to rim.

45. Turn hat over. Smooth clay from center of 2" circle to rim, hollowing out some of 2" circle center.

46. Remove more clay from hat inside. Shape until it fits.

47. Turn one rim side up. Allow hat to dry completely.

48. With serrated clay tool, apply paste to bird body, wings, and head. Skip legs, feet, and beak. Set aside to dry.

49. When texture has dried, sand legs, feet, beak, and hat smooth.

50. Paint textured parts Wedgewood Blue.

51. Over blue, dry brush Light Buttermilk wash, followed by dry brush of Raw Sienna wash.

52. Wash Wedgewood Blue back over textured areas. Dry brush Light Buttermilk wash, followed by dry brush of Raw Sienna wash again.

53. Mix Canyon Orange and Buttermilk 50/50, paint legs, feet and beak.

54. Paint Canyon Orange over mix. This color is translucent. Brush as smoothly as possible.

55. Wash Deep Burgundy then Golden Straw over orange.

56. Paint hat Deep Burgundy.

57. Wash Light Buttermilk, then wash Raw Sienna over hat.

58. Wash Deep Burgundy over hat.

59. Repeat any washes until satisfied with results.

60. Slide feathers through button loop.

61. Glue embellishments to hat. Glue hat to head.

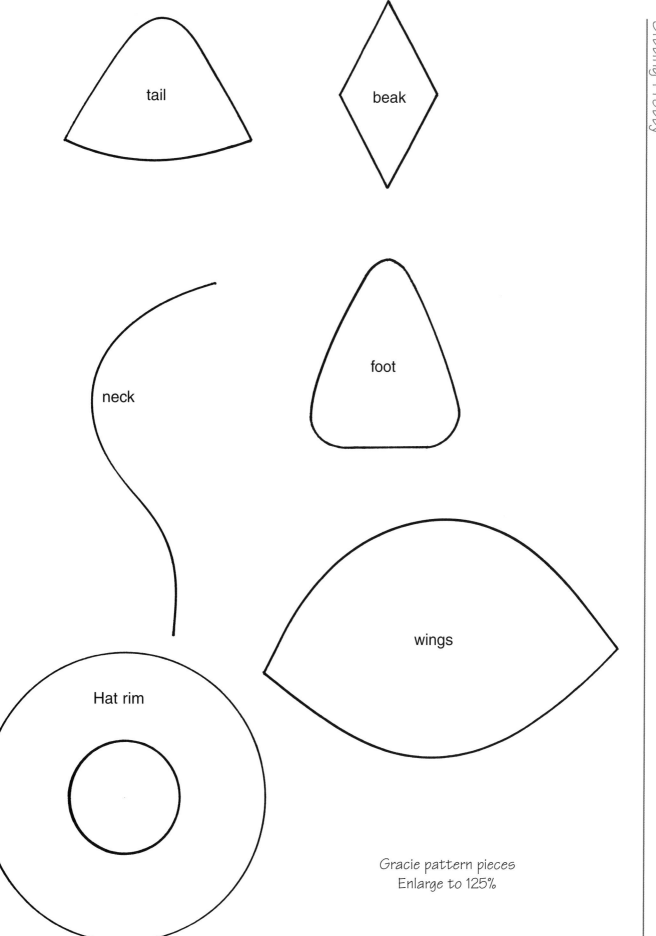

tail

beak

neck

foot

Hat rim

wings

Gracie pattern pieces
Enlarge to 125%

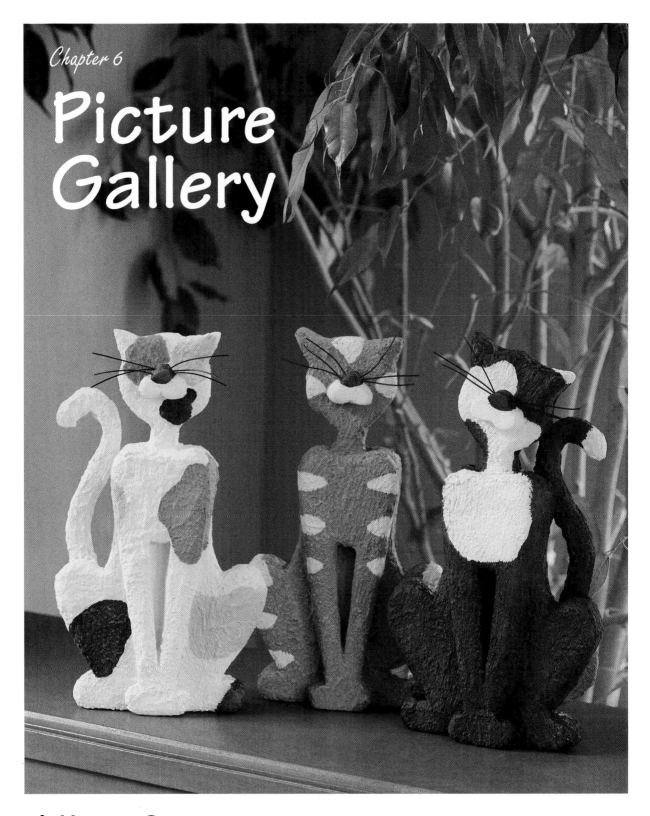

Chapter 6
Picture Gallery

Alley Cats

The instructions for the Black and Cream cat can be found in Chapter 5. The new cats have their heads on straight but their tails are different. One is switched to the other side, and for the other; a new tail pattern (elongated "C") was created.

Western Frame

The foam base for this frame was fashioned like the rest of the frames in Chapter 2. Joint compound was brushed on roughly. Copper rivets, copper wire (bent to form a "U"), and leather lacing are used to embellish the frame. Suede was cut for the mat.

Tall Vase Candle Pedestals

The two taller pedestals grew from the Vase Pedestal (shortest one) from Chapter 2.

Old Rooster

This is the second design I created using paperclay over foam. The body and head are balls. The rest of the detail comes from clay forms.

Patches

This project used some of the same skills found in Chapter 5: hind legs from the Dinosaur Named Drake, front legs from Gracie, and ears from the Cow Herd.

The Girls

Liz, Carla, and Sherry are enjoying some girl time. Sounds like they are talking about the great times they had with Gracie (Chapter 5) before she ran off to the city.

Large Pear

A solid block was created by gluing rectangles of 1" foam together. Once the glue dried, the block was sanded in the same fashion as the eggs in Row of Pears (Chapter 3) to create the pear shape.

Fruit Plaque

Foam was shaped by sanding an egg for the pear (Row of Pears Chapter 3) and balls for the cherries and apple.

Tommy's Lizard

This comes from the hands of guest creator Tommy Russell. At age 11, he learned how hot a hot knife really is, and that a smooth finish takes more patience than a boy his age has—and if you can think it, you can create it. It was created with the same steps as Stanley the Tree Frog (Chapter 3).

Maggie's Lady Bug Phoebe

Maggie's Ladybug guest creator, Maggie Russell, smiled the whole time this cute bug was in her hands. Her comment: "Wow mom, I see why you love your job so much!" At 12 years of age, she could handle all the skills that this project requires even though she was leery of cutting the large ball. Six balls are cut in half, glued together, and covered in paperclay for this creation.

Sources

Main Products

Foam
STYROFOAM® brand foam
www.styrofoamcrafts.com

Paperclay
Creative Paperclay® Company, Inc.
79 Daily Drive, Suite 101
Camarillo, CA 93010
(805) 484-6648
www.paperclay.com

Joint Compound
Plus 3™ Sheetrock® Lightweight All Purpose
Joint Compound
United States Gypsum Company
125 South Franklin Street
Chicago, IL 60606-4678

Foam Glue
Hold the Foam™
Beacon™ Adhesives
Signature Marketing
(800) 855-7283
www.beaconcreates.com

Acrylic Paints
Americana® and Dazzling Metallics®
DecoArt™
PO Box 386
Stanford, KY 40484
(606) 365-3193
www.decoart.com

Creative Versa-Tool™
Walnut Hollow Farm, Inc.
1409 State Road 23
Dodgeville, WI 53533
(800) 950-5101
www.walnuthollow.com

Individual Projects
Apple & Pear Clock
⅜" Clock Movement with Hands (#TQ500P)
Walnut Hollow Farm, Inc.
1409 State Road 23
Dodgeville, WI 53533
(800) 950-5101
www.walnuthollow.com

Fluttery Butterfly
Decoupage medium: Liquid Laminate™
Beacon™ Adhesives
Signature Marketing
(800) 855-7283
www.beacon.com

Gracie
Decorator Paste™
DecoArt™
PO Box 386
Stanford, KY 40484
(606) 365-3193
www.decoart.com

Feathers
Furnace Saddle Hackle 563-33
Mangelsen's
Omaha, NE 68127

14 Gauge galvanized steel wire
Steel wire is more rigid than other types. Steel
wire can be found at most home centers and
hardware stores.

Horse Frame
Decoupage medium: Liquid Laminate™
Beacon™ Adhesives
Signature Marketing
(800) 855-7283
www.beaconcreates.com

Letters
Krylon® Make it Stone!® Metallic Textured Paint
#8260 Gold
101 Prospect Ave. NW
Cleveland, OH 44115
(800) 4-KRYLON (800-457-9566)
www.krylon.com

Sunflower Clock
3/4" Clock Movement (#TQ710) & Clock Hands
(#1007B)
Walnut Hollow Farm, Inc.
1409 State Road 23
Dodgeville, WI 53533
(800) 950-5101
www.walnuthollow.com

About the Author

Koren's designs have been featured in multiple magazines and books throughout the last five years. Although she always thought of herself as creative, crafting wasn't always a part of her life. When she left her management career for a new endeavor (motherhood), crafting and creativity slowly became very important. After the birth of her second child, she felt the need for an outlet. Bowling with the girls on Thursdays wasn't enough. She needed something that didn't cost much or take her away from the kids.

During nap times, she began to decorate her home. She learned to hang wallpaper and fashion simple curtains. She taught herself faux and hand painting. As her discoveries and "can do" attitude grew, she felt the need to share the enthusiasm and fun. She began to do faux and decorative painting for hire. This put her in contact with a decorating magazine. After the magazine hired her as a project designer, the love affair grew stronger. She felt there couldn't be anything better in the world. She could continue to experiment and create then share the fun with others.

Koren, now an independent designer, would work 24 hour days if it weren't for the other thrills in her life: Her husband Gordy, children Maggie and Tommy, and getting dirty in her flowerbeds.

Koren can be reached at cfc@korenrussell.com

Photo by Heidi Lee, Appleton, Wisconsin

Hundreds of Home Décor Projects You Can Make

Foam Décor

Carve 30 Elegant Home Accents

by Kristy McNeil

Learn how to transform ordinary Plastifoam® into incredible architectural pieces. The result is so elegant that no one will suspect it's made out of foam. You'll see how to make everything from a French Ironwork Planter to a Gothic face oil lamp, floor fountain, and birdbath. These 30 foam projects look expensive, but are surprisingly economical and lightweight. Follow each project through step-by-step photography.

Softcover • 8¼x10⅞ • 96 pages • 100 color photos
Item# **FOAMD** • $19.99

Liquid Polymer Clay

Fabulous New Techniques for Making Jewelry and Home Accents

by Ann Mitchell and Karen Mitchell

Apply new and original sculpting techniques with Liquid Sculpey® to create unique jewelry, accessories, and home décor items. Twenty-two projects show you how to combine polymer clay with beads, metal filigree, and antique glass cabochons. Learn how each of the techniques developed and the medium or art application that inspired it. Step-by-step photos will easily guide you to completion.

Softcover • 8¼x10⅞ • 144 pages • 300+ color photos
Item# **LIQPC** • $21.99

The Handmade Basket Book

by Rebecca Board

Make beautiful baskets for your home with treasures from nature! You'll find step-by-step instructions for 15 projects for weaving willow, rushes, grasses and leaves into stunning wreaths, mats, baskets and more! they make stylish accessories for the modern home, as well as ideal storage containers.

Softcover • 9 x 10 • 80 pages • 120 color photos
Item# **HMBSK** • $14.95

Plaster Mosaics

New Technique As Easy As Spread, Paint, Carve

by Kristin Peck

Use plaster to create mosaic-looking works of art that will foll all but the most discerning eye. Use simple techniques to apply common plaster compound to different surfaces, from boxes and frames to furniture. Enjoy the beauty and elegance of these 16 easily made and inexpensive projects, including a serving tray, cabinet, door hanger, flowerpot, and chalkboard. Step-by-step photos and helpful sidebars make creating mosaics fun and easy!

Softcover • 8¼x10⅞ • 128 pages • 250+ color photos
Item# **MOSAI** • $19.99

Creative Containers

The Resourceful Crafter's Guide

by Jill Evans

How many times have you heard "One man's trash is another man's treasure?" Well, in this new book, author Jill Evans shows you how to turn your trash into beautiful home décor items, useful containers and earth-friendly gifts. From things like tuna cans, vegetable cans and cookie tins, you'll create 50 unique projects such as a scarecrow, red-nosed reindeer, penguin, candleholder and leprechaun!

Softcover • 8¼x10⅞ • 96 pages • 75 color photos
Item# **CRCONT** • $14.95

Felt Art Accents for the Home

44 Elegant, Yet Easy, Projects

by Trice Boerens

When you're creating projects to display throughout your home, felt will add sophistication to any home decorating project. Use such techniques as embroidery, appliqué, whip stitching, and stenciling to complete more than 40 projects, including pillows, table runners, photo frames, and much more. Easily follow step-by-step instructions as detailed in lavish accompanying photos. felt is not just for kids' crafts anymore!

Softcover • 8¼x10⅞ • 128 pages
165 color photos, 85 diagrams, 75 patterns
Item# **FAAH** • $19.99